合気忍術

第一巻　保護者道

AIKI NINJUTSU

Volume 1: Path of the Protector

Publishers' Graphics
140 Della Ct.
Carol Stream, IL 60188

This book is dedicated to all of those who have walked the warrior path throughout the centuries and those who are now following in their footsteps.

AUTHOR'S NOTE

Banzenkan Aiki Ninjutsu is a martial art that is effective for men and women of all ages, sizes and levels of athletic ability. The art is a perfect fit for anyone who decides to become a student, because of the art's use of using the attacker's energy against them, instead of relying on applying more force than the attacker.

The Ninja side of our lineage has a history of powerful women agents called ***Kunoichi***. These women were taught effective martial arts techniques to eliminate, subdue or escape a larger attacker as well as espionage techniques on how to gather information from people that might not let their guard down for a male agent.

This book will teach the fundamental techniques of Aiki Ninjutsu that will work for both men and women. There are no specific techniques that are gender specific.

Unfortunately, the English language makes it difficult when it comes to addressing both men and women at the same time, as there is no grammatically correct pronoun that is not gender specific. For the ease of reading and to keep the flow of the material moving, I have chosen to use the male pronouns of "he", "his" and "him." This is not meant to discriminate against our female warriors. Please know that every "he" should be read as "she" and every "his" or "him" should be read as "hers" or "her" depending on who is reading at the time.

I hope this book gives you many new "tools" for your "toolbox" and helps you take your training to the next level whether you are a ***Kunoichi*** (female ninja) or a ***Shinobi*** (male ninja).

- *Michael Jutoshi Eichenberg*

TABLE OF CONTENTS

INTRODUCTION

The history of the Japanese Samurai and Ninja warriors is one mired in bloodshed and polished with honor and mastery. Many would agree that they have set the standard for what true combat warriors should be. Today's modern military units strive to hold true to an ethical code of honor as well as train to be the most efficient fighting force they can be by utilizing tactics that were once used by these legendary masters. From the battlefield strategies employed by the Army and Marines to the stealth, camouflage, infiltration and escape and evasion techniques used by the special ops teams such as Army Special Forces, Navy SEALs and USMC Force Recon, we can still see the influence these amazing warriors have even on the high tech battlefields of today.

The deadly tactics and techniques utilized by the Samurai and Ninja work well on the battlefield because that is where they were born and perfected. So why should a person who lives in peacetime and does not find himself in warlike conditions practice these arts? Do they have a purpose for the everyday person?

The truth is that the principles and techniques utilized by these ancient warriors of Japan provide the perfect systems for personal protection and protection of our loved ones and those who might need our help. They were designed for eliminating a threat quickly and efficiently when the outcome could mean maiming or even death. The art of not using the skills learned, unless as a last resort, is the true goal of the warrior. This mindset and training make them the ideal art for the modern day protector/warrior.

In Banzenkan Aiki Ninjutsu, the definition of the word warrior is "an empowered and compassionate protector of self and others." This implies that a warrior is a person who learns not only the physical skills necessary to defend his own life, but also defend those who may need protecting, while at the same time learning all they can about who they truly are and how to live their life in a connected and loving way with everyone around them. This is a tall order and takes a lifetime of hard physical training and a deep introspection.

There are thousands of martial art styles from around the world. Every culture throughout history has developed systems to teach their military troops the necessary skills needed to survive in combat. Many of these have become antiquated and taught purely for history's sake. Others have concentrated on specific physical skills and developed rules to allow the students to test their skills in sport competitions. Very few have remained true to the ideal of protecting one's life in a modern environment where there are no rules and the attacks have changed, due to the conditions of that particular society. To practice an art only as it was taught hundreds of years ago does not prepare the modern warrior for the dangerous situations that will present themselves in today's world.

> *"Set patterns, incapable of adaptability, of pliability, only offer a better cage. Truth is outside of all patterns." - Bruce Lee, Tao of Jeet Kune Do.*

Even worse is to create an art that has no historical reference and is based solely on hypothetical assumptions with no basis in proven life or death combat, but only sport "combat" that has rules and regulations to protect the participants. This can give the warrior false confidence, making him believe that his art is real when in reality it will fail under the stress of the intense intention found in a life or death situation.

The art of Aiki Ninjutsu is one that has both history and lineage, over 2000 years, proven on the battlefield and in other life and death situations and adapted to fit the physical attacks that one would encounter in today's world. The secrets that made this art one of the few to survive into the modern era without having to become a historical exercise or sport are what make this art one of the best for the modern day protector. It is the emphasis on not relying on speed and strength as well as the mental aspects of becoming a more actualized human being, who understands self and others, that separates this art from those that are considered self-defense systems. Without the mental training, the protector may find himself in moral and ethical situations that end badly because he is controlled by ego instead of allowing compassion for all living beings to dictate his responses under stress.

All of the principles and secrets found in Aiki Ninjutsu have a physical and mental side. It is imperative that the student understands both aspects. It is unlikely that a modern day warrior will run into an attacker with a 3-foot long razor-sharp sword, but they will have to deal with people on a daily basis. For that reason, it is even more important that the Aiki Ninjutsu student understands that the mental training should constitute at least half of their training in the martial arts. This is the training that will give the warrior the "edge" in life allowing him to guide others so that the warrior can achieve the goals he has set to help make his life the best it can be.

All warrior cultures have lived by a set of rules and codes. The code of the Samurai is by far the most famous one. This code, called Bushido, listed the dos and don'ts of being an honorable warrior. In Aiki Ninjutsu, students have a success plan called the Student Creed and a code to live by called the Code of Mindful Action. Let's take a look at these important lessons that give the warrior the tools to take control of their everyday life.

STUDENT CREED

Ji-Shin: I believe in myself. I am confident. I can accomplish my goals.

Tan-Ren: I believe in what I study. I am disciplined. I am ready to learn and advance.

Son-Kei: I believe in my teachers. I show respect for all who help me progress.

The Banzenkan warrior follows a creed that teaches how to be successful at everything he does. This is a three step plan on how to achieve the goals that are necessary to make the warrior's life the best it can be.

First, the warrior needs to have confidence and belief that he can do what it is he wants to accomplish.

Second, the warrior needs to have a realistic plan and the self-discipline to follow that plan.

Third, the warrior needs to have powerful allies to help him achieve his goals. This is done by showing people respect so that they want to help the warrior succeed. This stage also involves the use of positive and negative role models. Positive role models are those who have accomplished what the warrior is seeking. Negative role models are people who exhibit the characteristics that would keep the warrior from being successful. These are people who show the warrior what will happen if he doesn't change the behavior that would keep him from attaining his goals. By using both positive and negative role models, the warrior can learn what he needs to achieve so that he can make the world a better place.

WARRIOR CODE OF MINDFUL ACTION

The Banzenkan warrior also utilizes the Warrior Code of Mindful Action created by To-shin Do An-shu, Stephen K. Hayes. This is a code that highlights the actions that are needed for the warrior to become a ***Tatsujin*** or completely actualized person of accomplishment. This code is something that the warrior student not only memorizes but works on at each ***kyu*** (color belt) level. By concentrating on these codes, the warrior is able to become a more positive and beneficial member of society.

The first 2 points deal with material considerations (White Belt)

- I protect life and health.
  I avoid violence whenever possible.
- I respect the property and space of all.
  I avoid taking what has not been offered.

The next 3 points remind you to be true to yourself (Yellow & Orange Belt)

- I develop significant relationships.
  I avoid abusing others for selfish gain.
- I thoughtfully express the truth.
  I avoid the confusion of dishonest words.
- I cultivate a positive attitude, a healthy body, and a clear mind.
  I avoid whatever would reduce my physical or mental well-being.

The next 3 points guide communication interactions with others (Purple & Blue Belt)

- I communicate health, happiness, and peace of mind to everyone I meet.
  I avoid violent, disturbing, and unduly critical speech.
- I promote harmony and positive momentum to bring out the best in everyone.
  I avoid causing alienation, doubt, and division among others.
- I encourage all to speak purposefully from the heart.
  I avoid the dull contentment of gossip and small talk.

The next 3 points are keys for operating effectively in the world (Green & Red Belt)

- I am as enthusiastic about others' fulfillment as I am about my own.
  I avoid treating others' successes as the cause of my lacks.
- I promote the enjoyment of life, and encourage others with my smile.
  I avoid setting myself against the world.
- I promote the search for personal realization of truth.
  I avoid the seductive comfort of narrow-mindedness.

The final 3 points suggest how to generate accomplishment (Brown/Black Belt)

- I accomplish what must be done in a timely and effective way.
  I avoid putting off doing that which will benefit me and my world today.
- I strive to be so strong that nothing can disturb my peace of mind.
  I avoid the negative effects of worry, doubt, and regret.
- I work to build love, happiness, and loyalty among all the members of my family.
  I avoid putting temporary personal benefit ahead of the welfare of those I love.

DOJO ETIQUETTE

In Japanese martial arts, it is traditional for the warrior to bow to the space they will be training in, the ***kamiza*** or front wall showing respect to the lineage, instructor and fellow training partners. It is customary to bow when entering the dojo as well as when leaving. This is also the case when entering or exiting the training floor. This method of bowing has no religious meaning. It is purely an Eastern way of showing respect. When performing the bow, the warrior should place their open hands at their hips with their heels touching and their feet opened up. The bow itself should be done by bending at the waist down to about a 45 degree angle. It is traditional to bow a little lower to someone who is elder or higher rank than you.

A standing bow, or ritsu rei.

A kneeling bow, or za rei.

At Banzenkan dojos, there are other forms of etiquette that should be followed. Here is a list of some of the most important items:

- Arrive on time for your classes.
- Always wear a clean uniform (gi) with matching t-shirt and socks.
- Always use a deodorant of some kind.
- Store your shoes and belongings in the appropriate spaces.
- No loud talking when not participating on the mat. This can make it very distracting to others who are training.
- Absolutely NO horseplay at any time is permitted. Safety is always number one at the dojo.
- Do not teach others unless you are a designated instructor. Be selfish of your time. It is not your responsibility to teach your training partner how to do the technique.
- No talking when the instructor is teaching.

It is important that students realize that they are the face of the dojo. How they treat people is how the dojo will be viewed by visitors and new students. Showing everyone respect by talking to others that are not in your friend group will create an atmosphere of community and the dojo will become a place of positivity that will change people's lives. Students should make sure they welcome everyone and spend time getting to know their fellow students. The dojo is a great source of networking for the warrior's lives inside and outside of the dojo.

WHAT DOES BANZENKAN MEAN?

万全館

Banzenkan is made up of three ***kanji*** (Japanese characters) that translate as the school or organization of flawlessness or perfection. Is it possible to be perfect? The obvious answer is no. True perfection is not attainable for a human being, but by training to be perfect the warrior will be closer to it than if they trained without that intention. The Banzenkan represents a system where the student trains so that he can master the art he is studying. This means he will understand intellectually the material as well as being physically able to perform the techniques, principles and secrets that are taught. One would think this is how all martial arts are taught, but that sadly is not the case. There are many black belt martial artists who do not know the names of the basic throws, locks and strikes or even the name of the style they study or what country it comes from.

Why is it important to know the names of things from another language? Simply put, it allows the warrior to communicate intelligently with other like-minded martial artists. Would you want to go to a brain surgeon who didn't know the names of the sections of the brain, of surgical instruments or what college he graduated from? Would you see him as an expert in his field? The same is true in martial arts. If the warrior wants to become a master martial artist then he needs to know more than how to just punch and kick. There may come a time when he will want to pass on his knowledge to others and to do that he must understand the material beyond just the physical techniques.

HOW DOES AIKI NINJUTSU TRANSLATE?

合氣忍術

The term ***Aiki*** is made up of two kanji that mean "Harmony" and "Energy or Spirit" and is often translated as "harmonious energy or interaction". ***Ninjutsu*** is made up of two kanji that mean "Perseverance" and "Art of". When all of the kanji are put together along with the word Banzenkan the complete translation is the "Organization of perfection by persevering through harmonious interaction."

The art of Banzenkan Aiki Ninjutsu teaches the warrior how to persevere in a physical attack as well as how to live his life in a way that sets him up, so he is not in a constant struggle just to survive, but is able to enjoy his life experience by being in harmony with everyone he encounters.

IMPORTANT LINEAGE OF AIKI NINJUTSU

There are many martial arts that exist today that come from the imagination of their creators which are not based on much authentic history and have never been proven on the battlefield. With the increasing popularity of the sport of MMA, mixed martial arts, it has become very common to try to pick and choose specific techniques from various martial arts that have no common philosophy, strategy or scientific application. This may work under a controlled and supervised sport situation with rules and referees, but may lead to tragic loss of life when employed in realistic life or death situations.

Banzenkan Aiki Ninjutsu is based on 12 different lineages, some of them as old as 2,000 years. These arts have been used by warriors in situations where they would be lost forever on the battlefield and if the techniques didn't work they would never be taught again. This historical lineage is important when the warrior is placing his life and the life of his loved ones on the line with no room for a second place finish.

Let's look at a few of the martial arts masters who dedicated their lives not only to learning the arts they studied but passing them on so that the students of Aiki Ninjutsu could have the amazing techniques, principles and secrets that make up the Banzenkan.

Sokaku Takeda

Sokaku Takeda, the founder of ***Daitō-ryū Jūjutsu***, which was later named ***Daitō-ryū Aikijūjutsu***, was born on October 10, 1859 and died on April 25, 1943 at the age of 83. His father, Sōkichi Takeda, was a samurai of the Takeda clan. It is believed that Sokaku began his training with his father at his dojo on their property. He attained the highest certificate in Hōzōin-ryū Takeda-ha and menkyo kaiden, license of total transmission, in Ono-ha Ittō-ryū, schools that focused on the use of the spear and sword, respectively.

His amazing and fearsome sword skills earned him the nickname of "the little demon of Aizu." He was only 150 cm (4'9") tall but it was said his skills reached a level of being almost godlike to the degree of being able to know a person's past, present and future without having met them before.

During his lifetime he taught about 30,000 students. These included martial artists who eventually founded other arts, such as Morihei Ueshiba, founder of Aikido and Hosaku Matsuda who was the teacher of Michiomi Nakano who founded Nippon Shorinji Kempo. Choi Yong-Sool, the founder of Hapkido, also claimed to be a student of Sokaku.

Morihei Ueshiba

Morihei Ueshiba was the founder of ***Aikido***. He was born on December 14, 1883 and died on April 26, 1969 at the age of 85. He was a student of Sokaku Takeda, founder of ***Daitō Ryū Aikijūjutsu***.

In 1903, he was not allowed into service in the Japanese army after failing the physical because it required him to be at least 5'2" tall. He stretched his spine by attaching heavy weights to his legs and hanging from tree branches. He retook the physical and was let in. He served during the Russo-Japanese War and was discharged in 1907.

He also studied in Gotō-ha Yagyū-ryū, Tenjin Shin'yō-ryū Jūjutsu and Judo under Kiyoichi Takagi.

As Ueshiba grew older his emphasis moved to making his art more circular and softer. Eventually, this included getting rid of the striking that was found in Daitō ryū. The art of Aikido itself went through various names, Aiki Jūjutsu, Ueshiba-ryū, Asahi-ryū, Aiki Budo and finally Aikido.

Morihei's son Kisshomaru Ueshiba became the Doshu, hereditary head, of Aikido after Morihei's death. Kisshomaru proceeded to spread the art of Aikido around the world making it one of the most practiced martial arts worldwide.

Morihei Ueshiba quotes:

> *"Failure is the key to success; each mistake teaches us something."*
>
> *"Even when called out by a single foe, remain on guard, for you are always surrounded by a host of enemies."*
>
> *"There are no contests in the Art of Peace. A true warrior is invincible because he or she contests with nothing. Defeat means to defeat the mind of contention that we harbor within."*
>
> *"Life is growth. If we stop growing, technically and spiritually, we are as good as dead."*
>
> *"All the principles of heaven and earth are living inside you. Life itself is truth, and this will never change. Everything in heaven and earth breathes. Breath is the thread that ties creation together."*

TOSHITSUGU TAKAMATSU

Toshitsugu Takamatsu was the 33rd Soke (Grandmaster) of ***Tōgakure Ryū Ninpō Taijūtsu***. He also held the title of Soke, grandmaster, in eight other martial traditions including: ***Kōtō-ryū Kōppō jūtsu, Gyokko-ryū Kosshi jūtsu, Kukishin-ryū Daken Taijūtsu, Kumagakure-ryū Ninpō, Tagaki Yoshin-ryū Jūtaijūtsu, Gikan-ryū Koppō jūtsu, Shinden Fudo-ryū Daken Taijūtsu and Gyokushin-ryū Ninpō.***

He was born on March 10, 1889 and died on April 2, 1972 at the age of 83. According to his own biography, he started training with Toda Shinryken Masamitsu in the arts of Kōtō-ryu Kōppō jūtsu and Tōgakure ryu Ninjutsu when he was only nine years old. At the age of fifteen he had a fight with two masters from the ***Musashi Ryu*** which ended with Toshitsugu suffering a ruptured eardrum. This eventually kept him from being able to enter the military.

At seventeen years old, he began training with Sensei Ishitani who taught him ***Kuki Happo Biken no Jutsu*** as well as other arts to include swords, bo staff and shuriken. Ishitani also trained him in the art of Ninjutsu.

Toshitsugu found himself in many fights, a lot of them to the death. His fierceness in battle earned him the nickname of the "Tiger of Mongolia." Some consider him to be the last authentic ninja due to his work in China, which some believe was for the Japanese government.

Toshitsugu was also the president of ***Minoku Seinen Botoku-kai*** association. This eventually became what is today known as the Budokan.

His most famous student was Masaaki Hatsumi.

Toshitsugu Takamatsu quotes:

> *"Let him cut your skin, and you cut his flesh. Let him cut your flesh, and you cut his bones. Let him cut your bones, and you cut off his life."*

> *"The way of the martial artist is the way of enduring, surviving and prevailing over all that would destroy him. More than delivering strikes and slashes, and deeper in significance than the simple outwitting of an enemy, Ninpō is the way of attaining that which we need while making the world a better place. The skill of the Ninja is the art of winning."*

Masaaki Hatsumi

Masaaki Hatsumi was born in Noda City, Chiba Prefecture, Japan on December 2, 1931 and is the 34th and current Soke of ***Tōgakure ryu Ninpō Taijūtsu***, (originally founded by Daisuke Nishina, who eventually changed his name to Daisuke Togakure.) Masaaki Hatsumi is the founder of the ***Bujinkan*** or "Hall of the Divine Warrior", which teaches his version of the nine systems passed on to him by Toshitsugu Takamatsu that he calls ***Bujinkan Budo Taijutsu***.

The art of ***Budo Taijutsu*** focuses on how to move the body in the most efficient way for real life encounters. This is a principle-based martial art versus a technique-based martial art such as Karate.

Masaaki Hatsumi also studied Aikido, Judo, Shito Ryu Karate and Kobudo. His most famous student is Stephen K. Hayes, founder of To-Shin Do.

Masaaki Hatsumi quotes:

> *"Your life is on the line. Practice well."*

> *"It is not a question of this technique working or that technique being cool. The most important thing is to survive."*

> *"You are not just fighting an opponent. You are fighting the unknown."*

> *"You can only understand if you've had the technique done to you. It's like food. You can't describe the taste, but if you've tasted it, you know what it is. You have to personally experience it to understand."*

> *"In avoiding and dodging, don't move too far; just enough is just enough. You get it, hm? But it's not your head that needs to understand!"*

> *"To become strong, powerful, or famous is really nothing special. People who seek seriously for a martial art with integrity, and having found it never leave it, are the protectors of true Ninjutsu…"*

Stephen K. Hayes

Stephen K. Hayes has spent his entire adult life in pursuit of perfection through the Asian martial arts and spiritual traditions. He traveled throughout Japan, Tibet, Nepal, and India to find the best of teachers. Grandmaster Masaaki Hatsumi, the 34th Soke of Togakure Ryu Ninpo Taijutsu, awarded him the extremely rare honor of 10th degree black belt in the historical Togakure Ryu ninja martial art tradition.

During his years in Japan, he used his professional acting skills in Japanese television and film projects. Most notable to Americans was his role alongside Richard Chamberlain and Toshiro Mifune in the NBC samurai epic Shogun.

He is the author of 21 books translating the timeless knowledge of the East into pragmatic lessons for contemporary Western life. His books have sold well over a million copies, and many of his volumes have been published in a variety of languages around the world.

In 1985, he was elected to the prestigious Black Belt Hall of Fame for his pioneering work teaching the legendary Japanese ninja martial arts.

In 1997, Stephen K. Hayes founded the martial art of To-Shin Do.

In 2006, Black Belt Magazine called him "One of the ten most influential living martial artists in the world."

He regularly served in the 1990s as personal protection escort and security advisor for Nobel Peace Prize laureate the Dalai Lama of Tibet.

Stephen K. Hayes with Tenzin Gyatso the 14th Dalai Lama

Stephen K. Hayes quotes:

> *"For the ninja, being powerful is the most loving thing he can do"*
>
> *"Do not speak to us of that which could have been. All that was is all that could have been. No More. No less. Let us level our gaze and move purposefully into today."*

The Banzenkan student is indebted to these incredible warriors who came before them and passed on the techniques and principles that comprise the art of Aiki Ninjutsu. Students show their respect by bowing to these master's photos before and after class.

SHOMITSU: THE SECRET OF BALANCE

The warrior understands that in a confrontation he will probably be at a disadvantage when it comes to size, strength, speed or skill. To even the odds, so that he can survive the encounter, the warrior needs to use the secret of taking his opponent off balance. When the human body is unbalanced the brain's first priority is to regain balance. This will give the warrior the time needed and the ability to defeat a physically superior opponent.

Figure 1

In many martial arts, the student is taught to assume a "horse stance" (figure 1) which is when the feet are placed on the same line with deeply bent knees. This stance is actually used to develop leg strength in the student but is sometimes misunderstood to be a position of superior balance. The truth is actually the opposite. By assuming the "horse stance" in an attack, the warrior is facing his weak direction of balance toward the attacker, making him the weakest he can possibly be.

The weak direction of balance can be found by drawing a line between the heels and a perpendicular line to that line, or more simply a plus sign between the heels. This is referred to as Shomitsu or the "first secret" in Banzenkan Aiki Ninjutsu.

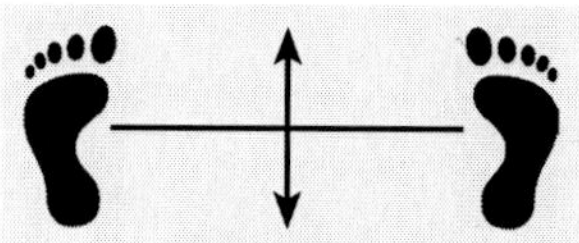

Figure 2

As can be seen in figure 2, this direction of balance goes to the front and the back. Because of this, if the warrior stands in a "horse stance" facing the attacker and the attacker strikes, pushes or bumps along the direction of the fore-and aft-line the warrior then will be off balance, making an effective defense almost impossible.

Instead of the "horse stance", the Aiki Ninjutsu practitioner will step back with his dominant side foot while keeping his toes pointing forward (figure 3). This will change the angle of weakness so that it is not putting the warrior in a disadvantaged position. The warrior understands that he can never entirely get rid of his weak direction of balance, but only hide it so that it cannot be used against him. He also understands that all feints, strikes and throws need to be used in the direction of the attacker's ***Shomitsu*** to be most effective.

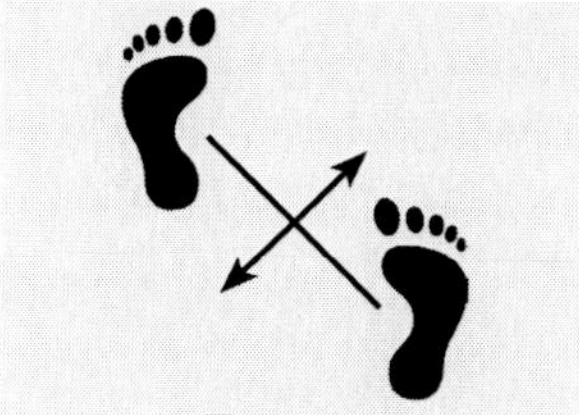

Figure 3

AIKI NINJUTSU POSTURES

In Aiki Ninjutsu, the warrior learns ***kamae*** or postures instead of stances. In a real encounter, the warrior must keep moving from position to position to stay safe and out of the reach of the larger attacker. This is why it is important that the warrior continuously move his feet. In many martial arts, the student assumes a "strong stance" and waits for the attacker to attack. This requires the martial artist to be much faster or stronger than his assailant, which is not usually the case outside of sport martial arts. When moving, the warrior is always looking to gain a tactical advantage over his assailant and not moving without specific purpose.

> *"The Way is in training... Do nothing which is not of value." - Miyamato Musashi, acclaimed Japanese swordsman and author of "The Book of Five Rings"*

The idea of kamae is for the warrior to bait an attacker to come in with an attack that the warrior has set up. This will make the defense much easier and puts the warrior ahead of the attacker instead of having always to respond. Kamae are not just how the warrior moves his feet but also where he holds his hands, which can influence whether the attacker strikes high or low, to the right or left side of the warrior. Kamae are used in unarmed combat as well as weapons training. The true warrior will learn to move from kamae to kamae to minimize the time that he is vulnerable to an unexpected attack.

In Aiki Ninjutsu, the warrior learns to respond to physical encounters by how he feels at the time. These are called attitudes or elements. There are four categories of element that make up the kihon or basic unarmed kamae.

The first is "Earth", which signifies a feeling either of extreme confidence or being in a confined environment: elevator, airplane aisle, up against a wall / car or protecting a loved one are just a few examples. These kamae and techniques are signified by their reliance on deeply bent knees, minimal footwork and an up and down motion.

The second element is called "Water". These kamae are used when the warrior feels threatened, intimidated or the need to get some space to figure the situation out. The kamae will have the warrior's feet in a 90-degree angle and make the warrior's torso as thin a target as possible. The techniques will utilize 45-degree angling to keep the warrior safe and open up the attacker's body for effective counterstrikes.

The third element or attitude is called "Fire". These kamae are used when the warrior is feeling assertive or a need to get through an attacker. These kamae and techniques will use the arms as shields to protect the head and body of the warrior as they move forward in a linear manner to steal away time and space from their attacker. These techniques require a good understanding and internalization of connection with the opponent.

The fourth element is called "Wind". These kamae give the opponent the illusion of vulnerability and non-aggression by the warrior. These techniques will use circular and spiral movement to subdue an assailant so that they cannot cause themselves or anyone else injury.

In an encounter, the warrior may switch from kamae to kamae as well as from element to element as the situation unfolds. There is no one element or kamae that is best for all situations.

Earth

- ***Shizen*** (Natural Posture); levels of awareness (1 & 2)

- ***Bobi no Kamae*** (Defense Ready Posture)

• *Seiza* (Seated Posture)

• *Fudoza* (Immovable Seat)

• *Hicho no Kamae* (Flying Bird Posture)

Water

- *Seigan no Kamae* ("Correct-Eye" Posture)

- *Ichimonji no Kamae* (Figure One Posture)

- *Doko no Kamae* (Angry Tiger Posture)

Fire

- *Jumonji no Kamae* (Figure Ten Posture)

- *Kosei no Kamae* (Attack Posture)

Wind

- *Hira no Kamae* (Flat Posture)

- *Hoko no Kamae* (Encircling Posture)

POWER TRIANGLE

The power triangle is assumed by placing the arms flat down by the warrior's sides, keeping the upper arms against the ribs, bring the hands together so that they meet in front of the spine. This alignment is where human arms are the strongest. An example of this can be seen when lifting weights. The closer the hands are together the stronger the warrior is. This is why he can bench press more weight than he can lift when doing pectoral flies.

The warrior understands that in a physical confrontation he may not be the biggest or strongest person. One way the warrior can help minimize this weakness is by making sure that when he punches, locks or throws the attacker he keeps his hands in his power triangle and the attacker's hands as far out of his power triangle as possible. This will ensure that the warrior is the strongest he can be and that the attacker is as weak as he can be. This doesn't mean that the warrior is now stronger than the attacker, but it helps even the warrior's strength deficit.

To maintain this more powerful position requires that the student move his lower body, from the hips, at the same time that he moves his torso, so that this alignment stays intact. This is one form of Taijutsu, art of using the body, to create power, instead of individual arm movement, which requires more muscle strength.

While practicing his techniques, the student can place rolled up socks or tennis balls under each armpit. If the item falls to the ground, then he has lifted his elbows away from his ribs and lost the advantage of the power triangle. This instant feedback will assist the warrior in internalizing the correct form needed for making his techniques the strongest they can be.

UKEMI

Almost everyone will slip and fall at some point in his life, so learning how to hit the ground safely is an important skill for the warrior. Besides this, the warrior student will take many throws during his training and must be able to receive them without injury. The word ***ukemi*** means "to receive." In the Banzenkan, the fundamental ukemi includes break falls, rolls and leaps. The Ukemi taught at white belt are as follows:

- *Zenpo Kaiten* – Front shoulder rolls (kneeling)

• *Zenpo Kaiten* – Front shoulder rolls (standing)

• *Ushiro Kaiten* – Back shoulder rolls (seated)

• *Ushiro Kaiten* – Back shoulder rolls (standing)

• *Yoko Kaiten* – Side rolls (kneeling)

• *Yoko Kaiten* – Side rolls (standing)

• *Zenpo no Ukemi* – Front break-fall (kneeling)

• ***Zenpo no Ukemi*** – Front break-fall (standing)

• ***Koho no Ukemi*** – Rear break-fall (seated)

- ***Koho no Ukemi*** – Rear break-fall (standing)

- ***Yoko no Ukemi*** – Side break-fall (seated)

- ***Yoko no Ukemi*** – Side break-fall (standing)

• ***Ten Tobi*** – "Heaven" or upward leap

• ***Chi Tobi*** – "Earth" or downward leap

- ***Zenpo Tobi*** – Forward leap

- ***Ushiro Tobi*** – Backward leap

- ***Migi Tobi*** – Right leap / ***Hidari Tobi*** – Left leap

The Banzenkan student must be able to perform these basic ukemi from a standing position before moving into the more advanced training classes. This is a safety requirement that ensures that he will have a long and enjoyable martial arts career.

More advanced ukemi such as rolling into a break-fall and handsprings are learned at higher belt levels.

HOKEN JUROPPO UCHI (Treasure fist sixteen strikes)

The beginning student of Banzenkan Aiki Ninjutsu will work on becoming proficient with the sixteen "treasure fists." These fists all utilize the concept of taijutsu, or "art of using the body." It is imperative that the warrior is able to create enough power to effectively take the balance and injure an attacker who is much larger than he is. This is accomplished by using unified body movement. A simple way of explaining this is that the warrior needs to move like a marionette puppet. The same side hand and foot must move together as if connected by a string, using body weight instead of muscle strength for power.

The warrior understands that by remaining relaxed he can generate more power than by tensing his muscles when striking. He never uses more tension in the arms and body than it would take to turn a door knob.

There are four things that must be done to create the maximum power available and at the same time set up skeletal alignment, ensuring the warrior does not bounce off of the attacker but instead forces the attacker backward off balance.

- *Use the legs.* This is done by bending or extending the knees as the strikes are applied. If the legs are left straight, then the warrior will lose balance easily and not be able to strike effectively.
- *Twist the spine.* The warrior understands that power comes from the twisting of the hips and not the movement of the arms. By adding this twisting, which begins in the hips and is extended through the rear leg, making a straight line from the striking weapon (fist, foot, etc.) to the leg, the warrior is able to send the energy of the strike through the target, maximizing the effect.
- *Breathing.* Under stress people will "tense up." This term is a literal translation of what the body does when scared. The weight rises up into the shoulder and chest area instead of being in the legs where it is more effective and they hold their breath. Just like lifting weights, the warrior must release this energy or Ki by breathing. This is best done as a beginner through a Kiai or "energy/spirit yell." In the Banzenkan, students are trained to use the word "HEY!" when striking. This allows them to breathe with each strike and generate energy with quick breaths originating at the diaphragm.
- *Intention.* The warrior must never pull punches or try to strike the surface of the target. He must extend his intention 6-8 inches through the target, effectively smashing it and knocking the attacker backwards. If the first three steps are used and the warrior consciously thinks of striking through the target, he will be able to generate enough energy to move and injure a much larger assailant.

"Don't hit at all if it is honorably possible to avoid hitting; but never hit soft."-
- Theodore Roosevelt

The list of the 16 treasure fists are as follows:

- ***Kikaku-ken*** ("Demon horn fist"; head butt)

- ***Shuki-ken*** ("Before the hand fist"; elbow strikes)

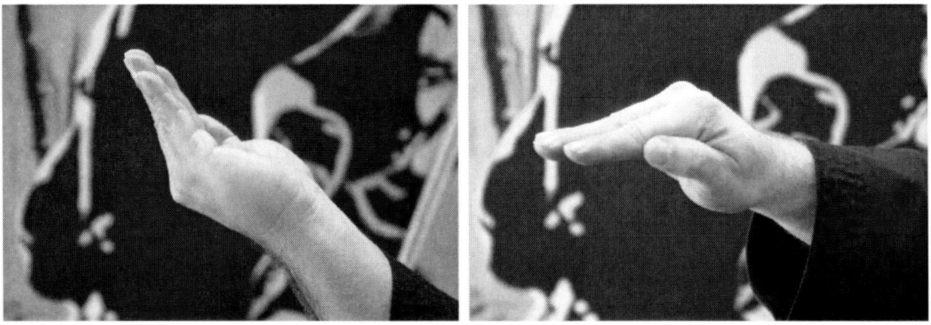

- ***Kiten-ken*** (Palm edge strike; also called a Shuto "sword hand")

- ***Fudo-ken*** ("Immovable fist"; clenched fist; also called a Kongo-ken "diamond fist")

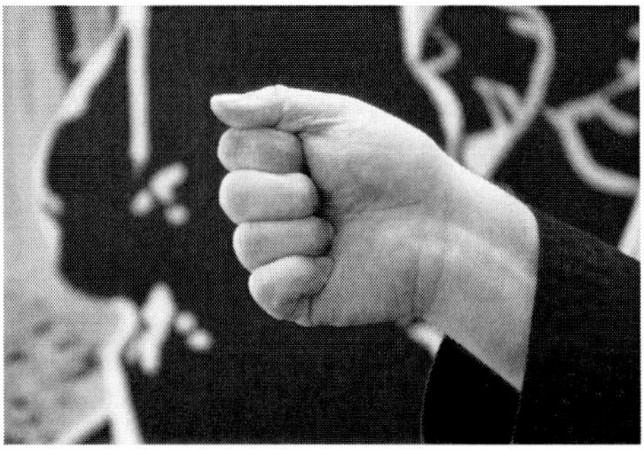

- ***Shito-ken*** (Thumb edge stab; also called a Boshi-ken "poking fist")

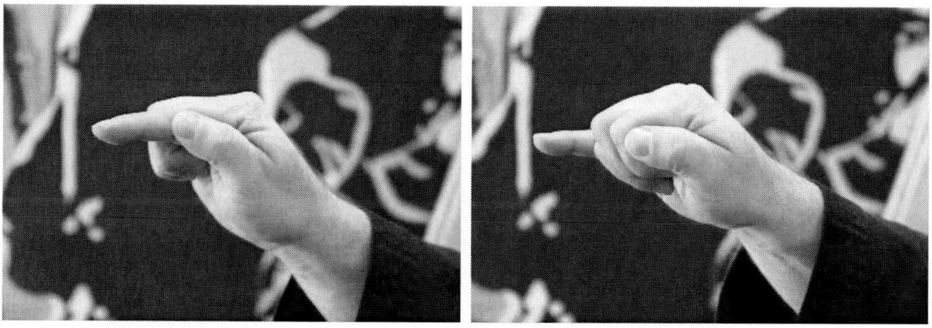

• ***Shishin-ken*** (Finger needle stab or poke)

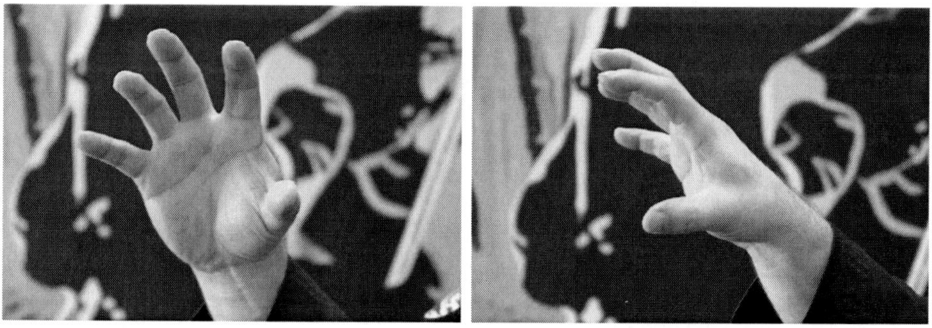

• ***Goshi-ken*** ("5 Finger Fist"; finger tip raking claw or stab)

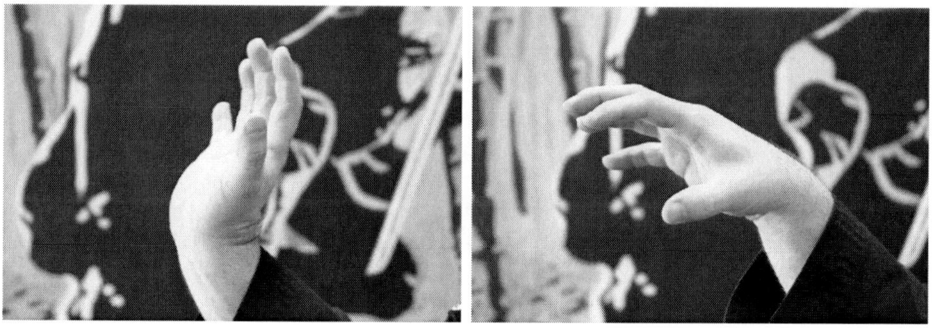

• ***Shako-ken*** (Palm strike followed by finger-tip claw)

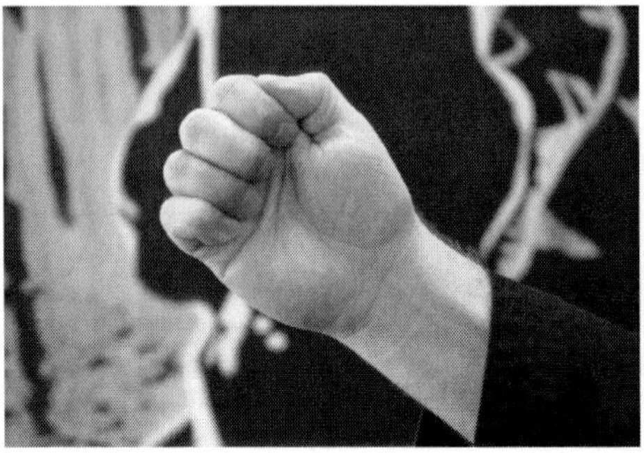

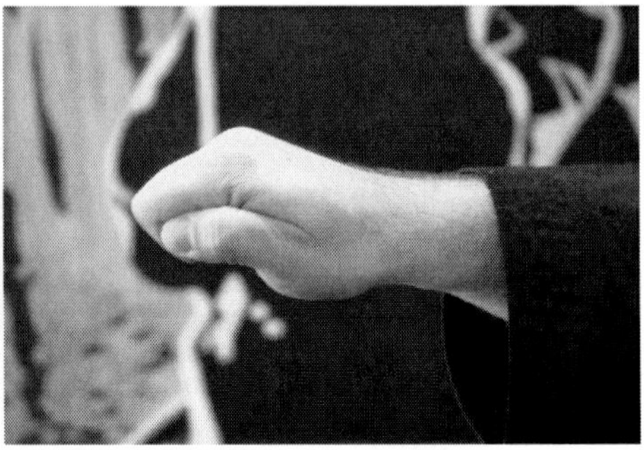

• ***Shikan-ken*** ("Finger house fist"; extended knuckle fist)

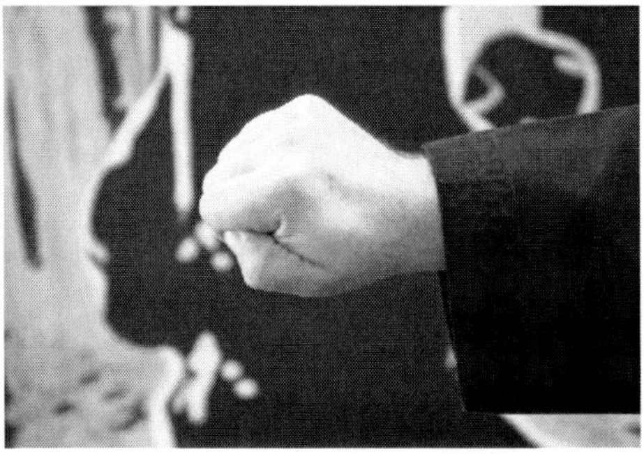

• ***Koppo-ken*** ("Bone breaking fist"; middle knuckle of the thumb fist)

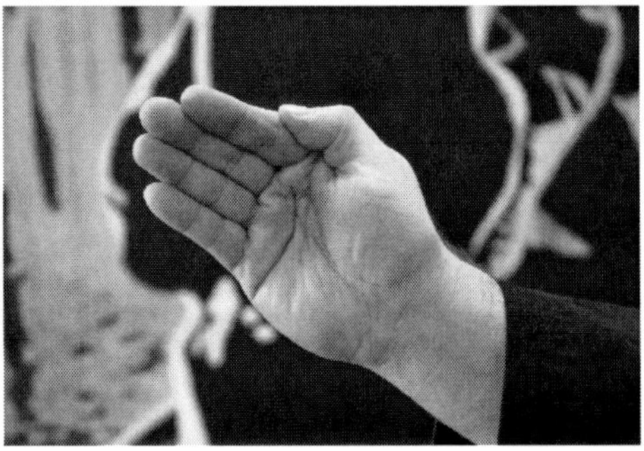

• ***Happa-ken*** ("8 leaves fist"; palm slapping strike)

• ***Ryu-ken*** ("Dragon fist"; extended middle knuckle of the middle finger fist)

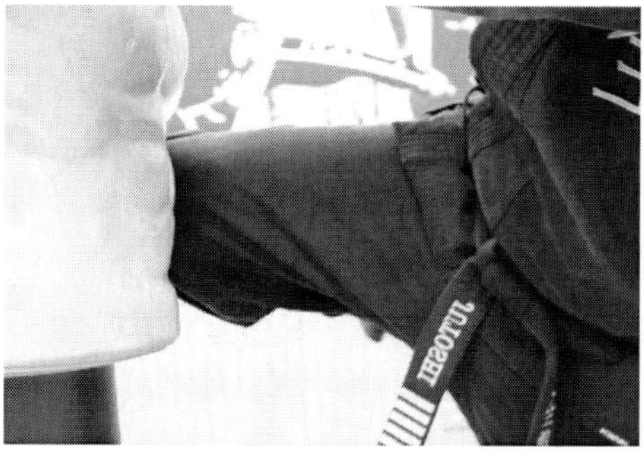

- ***Sokki-ken*** ("Before the foot fist"; knee strikes)

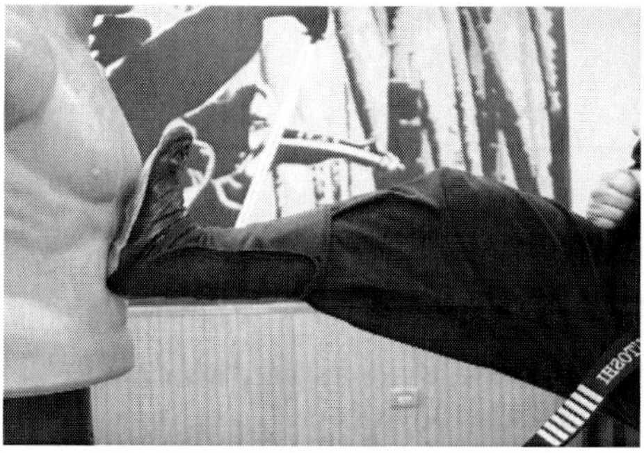

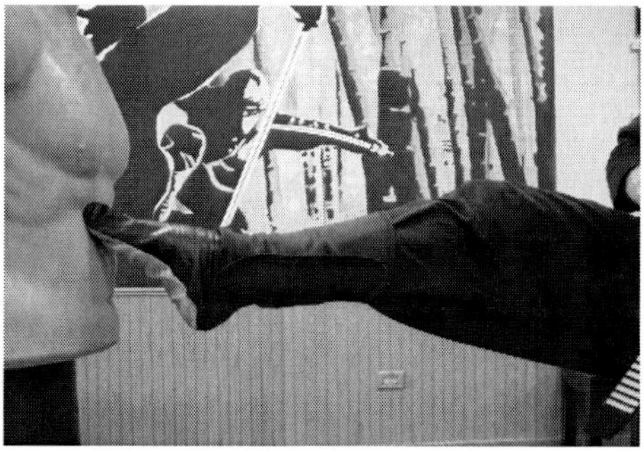

- ***Sokuyaku*** (Heel stamp kick)
- ***Sokugyaku*** (Toe stab kick)

- ***Tai Ken*** ("Body fist"; any other part of the body as a weapon)

  This last fist references using the warrior's body weight as a weapon when jumping or falling onto a downed attacker. This can also refer to any other body part that has not been specifically named as one of the sixteen treasure fists, examples; shins, forearms, shoulders, etc.

There are other strikes included in the fundamentals training of Banzenkan Aiki Ninjutsu. These include:

- ***Shitan-ken*** ("Finger end fist"; striking with the ends of all four fingers)
- ***Gyaku Tsuki*** ("Reverse punch"; cross punch)
- ***Choku Tsuki*** ("Lunge punch")
- ***Kikakshi Keri*** (Hidden kicks)
- ***Mawashi Geri*** (Roundhouse kick)
- ***Maegeri*** (Snap kick)
- ***Yoko Geri*** (Side kick)
- ***Shi-ho Geri*** ("Four directional kicks")

AIKI NINJUTSU PRINCIPLES

The art of Aiki Ninjutsu is made of twelve ***ryu-ha*** or martial systems from Japan. These include six that have Samurai lineage and six that have Ninja lineage. These systems have never been made into competition sport martial arts, but instead they focus on the dangers and solutions for a physical attack in the real world, where there are no rules or referees to ensure things don't become too dangerous.

Samurai Lineages

大東流 ***Daitō-ryū Aiki-jūjutsu*** – Great Eastern School

合気道 ***Aikidō*** – The Way of Harmonious Spirit

英信流 ***Eishin-ryū*** – Eishin School
(named after the 7th headmaster of the school)

九鬼神伝流 ***Kukishin-ryū Daken Taijutsu*** –
Tradition of Nine Demon Deities School

高木揚心流 ***Tagaki Yoshin-ryū Jūtaijutsu*** – High Tree Raise Heart School

神伝不動流 ***Shinden Fudo-ryū*** – Immovable Heart School

Ninja Lineages

戸隠忍法 ***Togakure-ryū Ninpō Taijutsu*** – Hidden Door School

虎倒流 ***Kotō-ryū Koppō Jutsu*** – Tiger Knockdown School

玉虎流 ***Gyokko-ryū Kosshi Jutsu*** – Jeweled Tiger School

雲隠流 ***Kumagakure-ryū Ninpō*** – Hidden Amongst the Clouds School

義鑑流 ***Gikan-ryū Koppō Jutsu*** – Truth, Loyalty and Justice School

玉心流 ***Gyokushin-ryū Ninpō*** – Jeweled Spirit School

The *Aiki* (harmonious energy or spirit) side of Aiki Ninjutsu is based on two different systems, Daitō-ryū Aiki-jūjutsu, and Aikido. These two ryu-ha represent the Yin of Yin/Yang (In in Japanese) "feminine" side of martial arts training. The emphasis is on the soft and circular movements that harmonize with the assailant's energy instead of using force on force to subdue an opponent. This side of training teaches the warrior the importance of the relationship between him and his opponent, as well as with the universe around him.

The *Ninjutsu* (art of perseverance) side of Aiki Ninjutsu is based on the 9 ryu ha that make up the Bujinkan system of Budo Taijutsu. These represent the Yang or Yo "masculine" side of training, is characterized by linear angles that open up targets to allow powerful strikes and locks. This side of training concentrates on the inner thoughts as well as the physical movements or taijutsu of the student. This "self-centered" side creates an awareness of self that helps the warrior become mentally strong and able to withstand conditions that would make most people surrender or quit.

Each side of training has a set of 8 techniques that get across the gokui (essence) of that mindset. These are called the ***Aiki Kihon Happo*** and the ***Ninpo Kihon Happo***. Each of these kata teaches a lesson that should be used in every technique the warrior does. The emphasis at the white belt level is the Aiki Kihon Happo, or "eight fundamental techniques of harmonious energy." These teach the warrior student how to use his spatial relationship, both mental and physical, to the attacker, to help guide him to a quick and efficient end to the conflict.

The Ninpo Kihon Happo or "eight fundamental techniques of perseverance" are taught at the 8th Kyu yellow belt level. These focus on how the warrior can move his body in a way that makes him the strongest he can be while at the same time opening up weaknesses in the opponent's attack that allows the warrior to win without superior strength or speed.

By learning and internalizing the Aiki and Ninpo Kihon Happo principles, the warrior has a fuller understanding of the Yin and Yang (In and Yo) aspects that are relevant in life as well as in a physical confrontation. To work on only one side limits the warrior in his decision making and will not give him the necessary skills to adapt to any situation. He will instead try to mold his emotions and skills to fit the situation. This essentially becomes the "square peg in a round hole" effect. To better prepare for any situation the warrior must understand how he relates to the world around him and how his own thoughts, words and actions can create the reality that he is living in.

AIKI KIHON HAPPO

The main idea of Aiki is to harmonize with the energy of the attacker. The easiest explanation for this is that if the opponent pushes, the warrior pulls and turns; if they pull, the warrior pushes and turns. The idea of using this Yin/Yang philosophy allows a much smaller defender to take control of an attacker's balance, giving him the chance to end the conflict without relying on using force-on-force.

There are eight additional lessons that need to be internalized from the Aiki side of Aiki Ninjutsu. By implementing all of them during a technique, the warrior can make any technique stronger and more powerful. These eight techniques are introduced on a mechanical level at white belt. The Banzenkan warrior student will learn to implement them against five different attacks; cross wrist grab, same side wrist grab, lapel grab, face punch and a kick to the chest.

The Aiki Kihon Happo techniques are all done from a posture called ***Bobi no Kamae*** or "Defensive Ready Position." This posture is assumed by stepping back with the dominant side foot with the feet shoulder-width apart. This will keep the warrior's weak direction of balance (Shomitsu) from being exploited from the front where the threat is. The warrior then pushes his hips forward so that the weight is on the balls of his feet with his heels slightly off of the ground. In a physical confrontation, the warrior must go forward, closing the gap to the attacker so as to take control of the situation. The longer it takes the warrior to end the conflict the worse the odds are that he will be able to do so.

Two things can happen in a physical attack. The assailant can take away the warrior's will to fight by hitting the warrior in such a way that he no longer wants to defend himself. For example, a hit to the groin or in the abdomen can make one unwilling or unable to move. There are mental defenses that can help the warrior overcome the desire to just lie down and hope the assault ends.

The other possibility is that the warrior could have the ability to defend himself taken away, by being knocked unconscious. This can lead to the warrior losing his life. The warrior must make sure that he protects his head so that he is not easily knocked out, by holding his hands in fists next to the sides of his head to deflect or absorb blows.

In the following, step-by-step descriptions of how to apply specific techniques are interspersed examples of how the concept embodied in the technique can also be applied to non-combat life situations. For simplicity, most of the descriptions are given for a right-handed attacker. Make the appropriate adjustments to apply the same technique to a left-handed attacker.Additional adjustments are required to respond to other forms of attack (punch, kick, lapel grab, etc.).

1. IKKYO (First Lesson) – Enter or close the distance
Muso Dori – "Incomparable Catch"

The first and most difficult lesson of this set is ***Ikkyo*** (first lesson), which teaches the student to enter or close the distance to the assailant. In a physical encounter, if the warrior uses his natural instinct to stay on line and back up to avoid being hit, he will end up being overpowered by a much larger and faster assailant. To make sure this doesn't happen, he must instead ***Irimi*** (enter) forward, off angle, and take the offensive as soon as possible.

In life it is important to realize that if one wants to be successful at anything one must give an effort and close the distance to one's goals. To simply wish for or complain about the lack of something will not bring one any closer to the desired result.

Uke (one who receives the technique) comes in with a cross-wrist grab to Tori's right wrist and pulls in (picture 2). ***Tori*** (defender) steps forward with his right foot onto Uke's Shomitsu while throwing a backhand strike to Uke's face with his captured hand (picture 3). Tori then steps in with left hand pushing Uke's right elbow to his right ear (pictures 4 & 5) and straightens out Uke's arm for an arm bar (picture 6). Tori finishes by applying a ***Tenkan*** pivot to take Uke down onto his stomach (picture 7).

合氣忍術

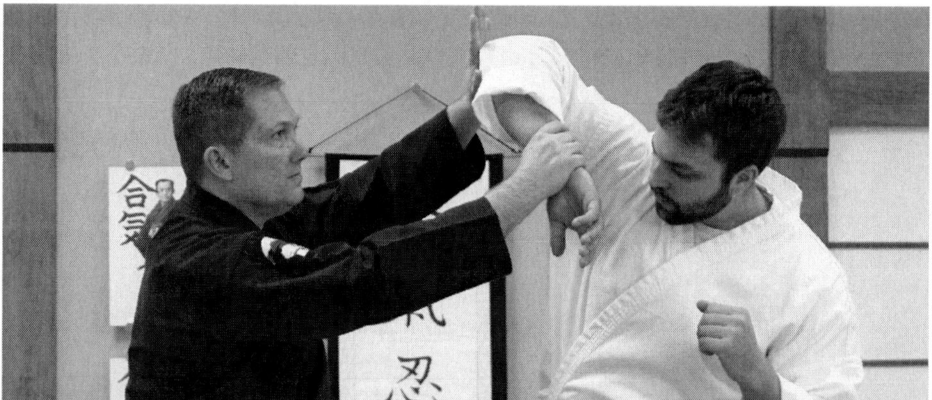

2. NIKYO (Second Lesson) – Set them up

Hon Gyaku – "Base Reversal"

The second lesson, ***Nikyo***, teaches the warrior to set up the attacker instead of trying to force his will on the situation. In the cross-wrist defense for Ikkyo, Uke grabs and either pushes or pulls, giving the defender, Tori, energy to use against him. In Nikyo, Uke grabs without pushing or pulling. To create movement and energy, the defender applies a wrist lock causing pain causing the assailant to pull away or attempt to push the defender away. This will give the warrior the energy he needs to apply an effective Muso Dori (Ikkyo) lock. This is also used as a "what if" to the first technique of Ikkyo. If the assailant pulls his hand to his chest as Ikkyo is applied, thus bending the elbow, the warrior will apply the wrist lock to cause pain, making the attacker pull away or extend the arm, again giving the energy needed to apply the arm bar from Ikkyo.

In life, it is important to find ways to set up situations so that the warrior can use people's natural reactions to help them "see the other side of things." By knowing how a person will react to what is said or done ahead of time, the warrior can say or do the right thing that will make the person they are dealing with respond with the needed action.

Uke comes in with a cross-wrist grab to Tori's right wrist (picture 1). Tori traps Uke's grabbing hand and does a clockwise turn with trapped hand applying wrist lock (pressure should be done as if putting fingers down Uke's throat) (pictures 2 & inset). Tori applies Ikkyo (picture 3-5)

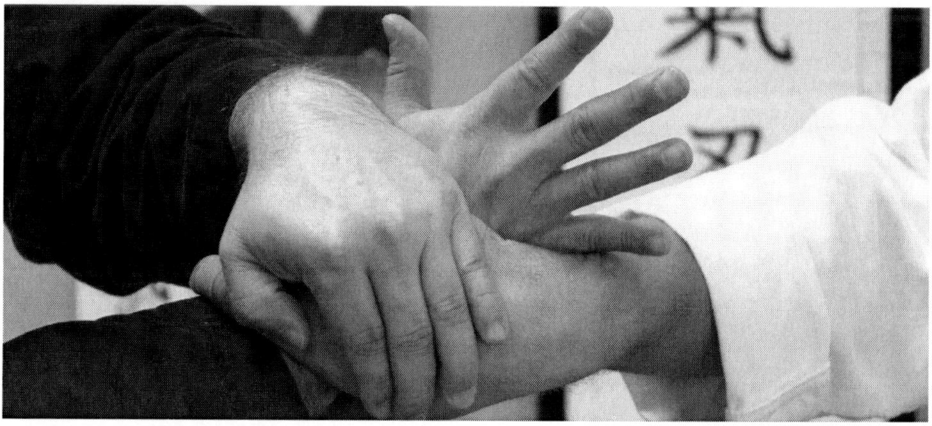

3. SANKYO (Third Lesson) – Go around the problem

Take Ori – "Breaking Bamboo"

In a physical encounter with a much larger, stronger or more determined attacker, the warrior must find a way to go around the energy of the attack so that there is no force-on-force needed. It is important to see the big picture and understand that what looks like the problem is not always the problem. A punch or kick coming at the warrior is not the real problem, the body throwing the punches and kicks is. The warrior must go around or under the attacking limbs instead of trying to stop them and counter. This will allow him to take control of the body, the real source of the threat.

In life, it is easy to get caught up in the details and not be able to see the big picture. Understanding the entire situation and what the real problems are is very important for the warrior. He must be able to find ways to go around obstacles to reach the real goals. A lot of times these obstacles are more mental than physical, which is why the warrior must spend equal amounts of time working on his inner-self as he does on the outer physical techniques of martial arts.

Uke comes in with a cross-wrist grab to Tori's right wrist and pulls Tori in (picture 1). Tori covers Uke's hand and steps in with right foot, hitting Uke's ribs with right elbow (picture 1-3). Tori pivots while putting on Take Ori wrist lock technique (pictures 4-6). Tori pushes Uke's elbow forward and down as he steps forward with the right foot (picture 7). Tori pivots, facing the opposite direction, and applies Muso Dori from the front (picture 8). Tori then lifts Uke's hand up and uses his arm as a "shovel handle" to push Uke down onto his face and chest (pictures 9-10).

4. YONKYO (Fourth Lesson) – Pain & indifference

Kunnuki – "Bolt Lock"

When studying a martial art it is important for the warrior to understand that he will have to cause pain in the dojo to another human being. Most people who come to study Aiki Ninjutsu are good people. They do not get into fights and are caring and loving individuals. The thought of injuring another person is not something they think of as normal. It is important that the warrior student understands that to stop an attacker he will have to cause pain and injury to the assailant. In the dojo, injury is NEVER acceptable. The student must learn to use body control to keep from injuring his training partners. All students come to the dojo to better themselves and will willingly give their bodies to their partners and expect that they will leave in the same physical condition in which they arrived. There is a difference between pain and injury. Pain stops once the technique has ended. Injury takes time and/or medical attention to heal.

The warrior student must learn to become indifferent towards causing others as well as to receiving pain. The only way to know if pressure points, joint locks and throws work is by doing them. Learning what the technique feels like reinforces the technique in the warrior's mind, making it more likely that he will use it in a confrontation.

In life, the warrior must learn to become indifferent towards the base negative emotions. Anger, jealousy and greed can cloud the warrior's outlook making it so he cannot see the truth, only his own distorted view point. To be a compassionate person towards everyone and everything is the ultimate goal towards becoming a Banzenkan master, and indifference is the first step on that path.

Tori applies Ikkyo (picture 1). Tori then applies Kunukki lock with the inside knuckle of his left index finger, causing pain, and pushes Uke down to the ground (picture 2 and inset)

合
氣
忍
術

合
氣

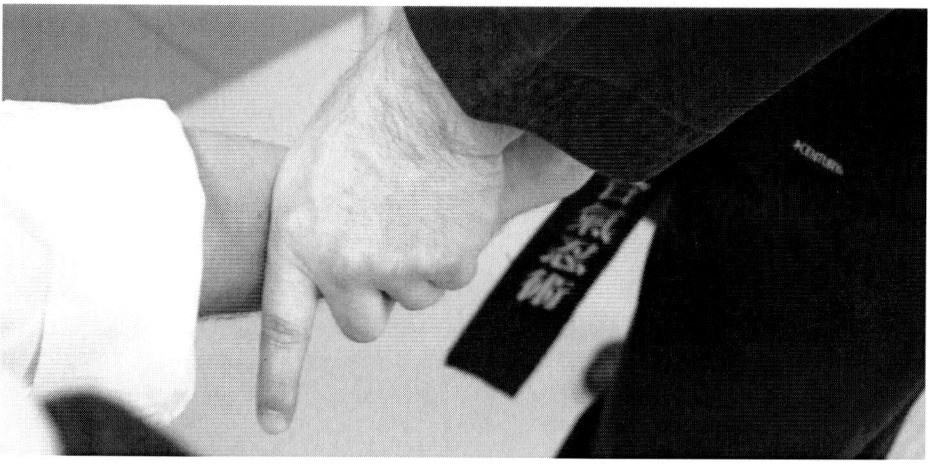

5. GOKYO (Fifth Lesson) – Strike in every technique
Omote Musha Dori – "Obvious Warrior Catch"

This lesson teaches the warrior that he must use striking to unbalance his opponent while setting up a powerful throw or joint manipulation. By striking, the warrior can not only take the aggressor's physical balance, but can interrupt the next attack by short circuiting the attacker's mental plan. The pain of being struck will break the connection that the assailant has with the defender and bring his attention inward towards himself. This will give the warrior time to apply the technique needed to end the confrontation.

The warrior should strike a minimum of three times to off-balance the opponent before trying to apply a lock or throw. This will confuse the attacker and put him on the defense.

In life, the warrior needs to make an effort every day to achieve their goals. He must do something daily to further his cause, bringing him closer to accomplishing this vision. Once he has decided on a goal he must stay connected with the outcome, working continuously towards the desired end.

Uke comes in with a cross-wrist grab to Tori's right wrist (picture 1). Tori pulls hand away from Uke and Yoko Aruki (side cross step) left in front of right and sweeps Uke's arm in a counter clockwise motion with Tori's left hand, grabbing Uke's wrist on the inside (picture 2). Tori steps in with his right foot and applies an Omote Shuto to Uke's neck (picture 3). Tori throws his left leg back and behind him as he applies an Omote Shuto takedown to Uke's right inner elbow putting Uke on his back (pictures 4-5). There is also an outside version that will be covered in classes with a qualified instructor.

合氣忍術

AIKI NINJUTSU

6. ROKKYO (Sixth Lesson) – Lead or guide your opponent

Ura Musha Dori – "Not So Obvious Warrior Catch"

The sixth lesson is one of off-balancing the attacker the moment contact is made. This is done by parrying the attack and guiding the attacker to a position of unbalance. By utilizing this principle, the warrior will be able to set the attacker up for a throw or lock that will require no effort, or get him to run into powerful strikes. If done properly, the technique should move the attacker by keeping him in front of the warrior's chest.

In life, learning how to guide and lead others to see the warrior's view point is a priceless skill. One way to do this is through the use of elements that we will discuss in a different chapter.

Uke comes in with a cross-wrist grab to Tori's right wrist and Tori shifts to the right, grabbing Uke's wrist by the inside with Tori's right hand (picture 1). Tori twists the wrist upwards and steps in with left foot as he puts his left hand on the top of Uke's right inner elbow, pushing down and forward (picture 2). Tori Tenkan pivots taking Uke to the ground (pictures 3-4)

7. NANAKYO (Seventh Lesson) – Become skin tight
Shiho Nage – "Four Directional Throw"

This lesson answers the question, "How far do I enter?" The answer is that the warrior must enter until there is no space between him and his attacker. A fight is really about space and who controls it. If nobody is in control of a space then the first one who moves in has the advantage. For this reason, the warrior must enter in and take up all of the space until he is "skin tight" against the attacker, giving the attacker no room to counter the warrior's technique.

In life, it is important to have powerful allies to help the warrior attain the things he needs to make his life the best it can be. One way to do this is to develop meaningful relationships with people. The warrior understands that taking people for granted and abusing others will not lead to a life of happiness. To have a truly enjoyable life experience, the warrior must have genuine relationships with those who are in his inner circle. Understanding, caring and loving are the secrets to living a fulfilled life.

Uke comes in with a cross-wrist grab to Tori's right wrist and Tori shifts to the right, grabbing Uke's wrist by the inside with Tori's right hand (picture 1). Tori steps in with left foot applying a rising arm bar with Tori's left arm (picture 2). Tori then Tenkan pivots under Uke's arm bending it so that Uke's hand is by his ear (pictures 3-4). Tori "cuts" down with Uke's trapped wrist throwing Uke to the ground (picture 5).

万全
AIKI NINJUTSU
USA
AIKIDO

8. HACHIKYO (Eighth Lesson) – Become the center

Irimi Nage – "Entering Throw"

This final Aiki lesson teaches the warrior that he must become the center of the technique. The secret is to use spiraling movements to generate power. By becoming the center of the technique, the warrior gets the attacker to orbit around him so that the attacker will run into powerful throws, joint locks and strikes. This creates a force and power that is way beyond that which can be generated by just the warrior alone.

In life, the warrior must understand that he is the center of his own universe. He is responsible for his life experience. Taking responsibility is the first step to living the life the warrior desires. If he cannot take responsibility, he will manifest excuses instead of solutions. To know that everything good or bad originates from the warrior himself is the first key to true life mastery.

Uke comes in with a cross-wrist grab to Tori's left wrist. Tori steps out to the right at a 45-degree angle and grabs Uke's left elbow with Tori's left hand and Uke's neck with Tori's right hand (Shoho Basho). Tori positions himself in the "dead space" (Shi Kaku) behind Uke (pictures 1-3). Tori steps back and does a Tenkan pivot as he brings Uke's left ear to Tori's left shoulder and Uke's left elbow to Tori's left hip (picture 4). As Uke runs to keep up (orbits), Tori places Uke's throat into the crook of his left elbow (picture 5 & inset). Tori pivots the opposite way, lifting his elbow to the ceiling throwing Uke on his head, back and shoulders (picture 6).

万全
合氣忍術

MOVE, HIT AND TURN

The eight principles or lessons of the Aiki Kihon Happo can be difficult to do while under the stress of a real attack. When exposed to stressors, the human body releases many chemicals to cope with danger, including adrenaline. This potent hormone combination makes it possible for the warrior to move faster, be stronger and endure more pain. These survival benefits unfortunately come with some severe side effects that include tunnel vision, hearing impairment and shaking hands. The brain slips from "thinking brain" into "survival brain." This may make it impossible for the warrior to access the files that contain the information he learned in the dojo.

How does the warrior make sure that he is applying all eight of the important principles when the conscious brain is not working at 100%? He must have a lot of repetitive practice that internalizes the lessons so that they become second nature. After lots of training, the warrior then needs to be put under stress to create neural pathways to the necessary information.

To make it a little easier, Aiki Ninjutsu has designed a three step procedure that uses all eight of the lessons from the Aiki Kihon Happo. These are called Move, Hit and Turn. The warrior should make sure that he first moves out of the way of the attack, strikes to interrupt the assailant's mind and physical balance and then turns to throw the attacker to the ground, causing an injury that will give the warrior time to escape.

Let's look at the Move, Hit and Turn concept in depth and how it incorporates all eight principles.

Move:

- The warrior must enter (Ikkyo) to close the distance between himself and his assailant in such a manner that goes around the attacker's energy (Sankyo) so that force-on-force is not needed.
- The warrior moves until he is skin tight (Nanakyo) with the assailant causing him to lock up or ***tsukuri***.

Hit:

- The warrior must strike in every technique (Gokyo) to cause pain (Yonkyo) which interrupts the attacker's mental, physical and spiritual balance (***Kuzushi***).
- The warrior strikes to enter (Irimi) and to set up the attacker (Nikyo) for a lock or throw.

Turn:

- Once the warrior has moved in and hit he must turn to lead the attacker (Rokkyo) into an effective lock, throw or strike.
- To create the most powerful technique the warrior must become the center of the turning circle (Hachikyo) to use centrifugal force instead of linear force-on-force.
- The warrior then executes the technique (***Kake***)

By using this simple system, the warrior can implement the eight Aiki Kihon Happo lessons as well as the Four Stages of a Technique (discussed in chapter 18) in every technique he performs, whether in the dojo or on the street.

NINPO KIHON HAPPO

The other side of Aiki Ninjutsu is the Ninpo side. This side refers to how the warrior feels and how he moves. There are eight additional lessons that the warrior should add to every technique to make him the absolute strongest he can be. These eight techniques were handed down on the Ninjutsu side to Soke Masaaki Hatsumi, the 34th Grandmaster of Togakure Ryu Ninpo Taijutsu, by his teacher Soke Toshitsugu Takamatsu, who said that they contained the very essence of Budo (warrior way).

This set of techniques concentrates on how the warrior thinks and moves his body. It is different from the Aiki Kihon Happo, which focused on how the warrior related to the attacker.

1. ICHIMONJI NO KATA – (Figure 1 Form)

Remain neutral & strike to the Shomitsu

This technique teaches the warrior the importance of not extending his balance too far in any direction. The warrior needs to be able to move in any direction at any given moment. This technique also focuses on teaching the warrior how to strike to the attacker's weak direction of balance also known as ***Shomitsu*** (First secret.)

In life, it is important to remain neutral so that the warrior can see different perspectives of any given situation. If one becomes too emotionally involved, one can get clouded by one's own opinions and unable to see what needs to be done to be effective. The warrior must also learn to maintain balance in his life. Being able to give the proper amount of time to career, personal relationships and self-development will make the warrior's life more interesting and productive.

Both Uke and Tori begin in Ichimonji no Kamae (picture 1). Uke throws a lunging right punch (picture 2). Tori shifts to the right, counterstriking Uke's arm with his left hand (pictures 2-5). Tori then shifts his left foot back and onto Uke's Shomitsu (picture 6), and then steps in with a right Omote Shuto to Uke's neck (picture 7).

合氣忍術

2. JUMONJI NO KATA (Figure 10 Form)

Spinal twist & follow the arm in

This technique teaches the warrior how to use the twisting of the spine and hips to generate power in all strikes and throws. When combined with bending the knees, this will make the warrior powerful when applying any technique. To do this correctly, concentrate on pivoting the feet. This keeps the warrior's hands in his power triangle.

The other lesson in this technique is that once there is tactile connection with the attacker's arm the warrior can follow the arm into pressure points located on the attacker's sides. These points will create a hot pain and override the attacker's mental processes, making him worry more about his own safety and not about injuring the warrior.

In life, the warrior practices good posture and movement so that he can maintain good health. Most injuries in the USA occur because of bad posture and uncoordinated movements.

Uke and Tori start in Jumonji no Kamae (picture 1). Uke throws a right punch and Tori spinal twists out of the way and counter punches underneath Uke's right elbow with a left Fudoken (picture 2 & inset 1). Tori then spinal twists the opposite way, driving a left hand Boshi ken into Uke's right Butsumetsu (picture 3 & inset 2). Tori ends by bringing his left hand up for a back hand rising hit to Uke's face (picture 4). Repeat on the opposite side.

合
忍
術

氣
忍
術
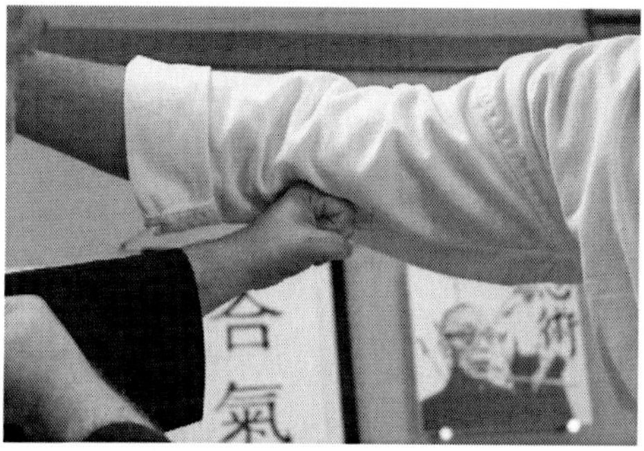
合
氣

忍
術
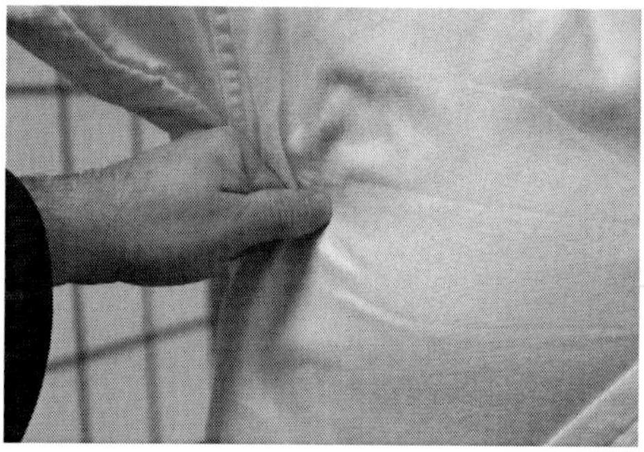

氣
忍
術

3. HICHO NO KATA (Flying Bird Form)

Expand and contract & maintain contact

This technique teaches the warrior that keeping the back straight and the knees bent creates a strong sense of balance. When striking or throwing, the warrior will use his body weight by moving his legs up and down in a coordinated motion with the technique.

Once the warrior makes any physical contact with the attacker, he must maintain that contact until it is tactically unsound to do so. This will allow the warrior to feel the movement and intentions of the attacker, letting him know what the attacker intends to do next. This skill is important because during a conflict the warrior's eyes can be attacked by things like chemical irritant spray, dirt or fingers, taking away the warrior's optical vision. By maintaining contact, the warrior can fight in darkness or when blindfolded.

In life, it is important for the warrior to maintain many contacts. The ninja warrior must be able to rely on the people around him for information and for assistance. The warrior understands the saying, "It is not what you know, but who you know that is important." The warrior realizes that it is impossible to be skilled in all areas, so there is a need to be surrounded by people who can provide guidance and help in areas where he may have weaknesses. This is one way to be strong, utilizing the skills of allies.

Uke begins in Ichimonji no Kamae and Tori in Hicho no Kamae (picture 1). Uke throws a lunging right lower punch. Tori performs a lower counter punch to Uke's attacking arm, while sinking his weight. (picture 2). Tori then kicks with a Sokugyaku (toe stab) to Uke's Suigetsu (picture 3). Tori steps down with left foot onto Uke's Shomitsu line (picture 4). Tori executes a lunging Ura Shuto to Uke's neck (picture 5).

AIKI NINJUTSU

4. OMOTE GYAKU DORI (Outer Reversal Catch)

Take what is given

In a physical confrontation, the warrior must use what the assailant is giving. It is very common in most martial arts to try to stop what the aggressor is doing, blocking the punch or kick, to open up a space for a counter attack. This requires the warrior to be faster and stronger than his attacker. Instead, the Banzenkan warrior realizes that he must use whatever the attacker is trying to implement against him. Instead of blocking a punch or knocking a grab away, the warrior will extend the attack, taking the assailant's balance and setting the assailant up for an effective counter. This mentality will make it so the warrior does not need to force his will upon his attacker, but instead allows the assailant's actions to bring about his own defeat.

In life, the warrior must learn to appreciate what he currently has. Many people spend their lives desiring things they don't have and never find happiness with the people and things they do have. It is a natural inclination of the ego to always want more. Knowing this, the warrior works on taking control of these urges and finds a life of fulfillment and peace. This principle is also the skill of being able to take a compliment and not always feeling the need to "one up" someone.

Uke steps in with a left hand grab to Tori's right lapel (picture 1). Tori shifts back into a left side forward Ichimonji no Kamae and hits with an Ura Shuto with his left hand to Uke's left temple (picture 2). Tori then shifts into a right side forward Ichimonji no Kamae as he uses his elbow to lift Uke's hand off of his lapel (picture 3). Tori finishes by shifting into a left side forward Ichimonji no Kamae applying an Omote Kotegaeshi (outer wrist turn) to Uke's grabbing left hand (pictures 4-5).

合氣忍術

5. OMOTE GYAKU TSUKI (Outer Reversal Strike)

Know more is coming

There is a tendency in martial arts to do a lot of one-step sparring where the attacker only comes in with one punch, one kick or attempts only one throw. The student then applies the technique he is working on. This does not prepare the warrior for real combat situations. In a real life encounter, the aggressor will continue to try to injure the warrior until he is successful or is stopped. Because of this mistake in training, a lot of martial artists find themselves on the "losing" end of a physical encounter on the street. The Banzenkan warrior student understands that "punches come in bunches" and they must prepare for the next attack.

In life, it is common for people to become complacent. They do not like change. The warrior realizes that nothing is static and that new experiences and being able to adapt is just a normal part of his existence. He understands that the bad times will pass as well as the good, and learns to expect and look forward to what life has to offer next.

This technique is almost exactly like Omote Gyaku Dori except that Uke grabs the lapel and throws a punch. Tori shifts back and strikes the inside of Uke's attacking arm instead of the temple (pictures 1-2). From here, Tori finishes exactly like Omote Gyaku Dori (pictures 3-5).

合氣忍術

6. URA GYAKU (Inner Reversal)

Build in a defense – Variation: HON GYAKU (Base Reversal)

Because the warrior understands that there is going to be more coming in an attack he must learn to build in a defense that interrupts the attacker's plan. This can be done by positioning the warrior's defense in a way that the aggressor runs into a lock or is taken to a place where, if he continues to attack, he will throw himself to the ground. This principle is called ***Tsukuri***, and is explored in a later chapter.

In life, the warrior must find ways to make sure he is not caught off guard. This can be done in relationships by learning how to control conversations. The saying "Never ask a question you do not know the answer to," is be a good example of building in a defense. "Knowledge is power" is another saying that fits this principle. The warrior must know more about the topic than the person he is dealing with, so that he can approach the situation from more than just one angle. This will set it up so the other person feels it was his idea instead of his becoming defensive and closing himself off to what the warrior needs to get accomplished.

Uke steps in with a left hand grab to Tori's right lapel. Tori shifts back into left side forward Ichimonji no Kamae and hits Uke with a left hand Happa-ken (slap) to the right side of Uke's face before covering Uke's grabbing hand with the left hand and pulling down with his elbow to unbalance Uke (picture 1). Tori turns his chest towards Uke, applying a horizontal Hon Gyaku lock that keeps Uke from coming back in. (picture 2). Tori steps in with his right foot with both thumbs on the back of Uke's hand turning the fingers forward while pushing Uke's hand towards his forehead and applying an Ura Kotegaeshi (inner wrist turn). Tori pivots to take Uke to the ground (pictures 3-6).

合氣忍術

7. MUSHA DORI (Warrior Catch)

Use your legs – Variation: ONI KUDAKI (Demon Crusher)

In a physical confrontation, the warrior must not forget to use his legs. Under stress, people tend to become hyper-focused on their hands and the attacker's weapons. The warrior must understand that he needs to move his feet as well as use kicks.

In life, the warrior must remember to see the big picture. It is easy to become blinded by one's own selfish interests and miss the opportunity to understand the truth. By moving to see a new perspective, the warrior is able to see what the situation needs instead of what the warrior wants to be true. This is addressed in the Code of Mindful Action under: "I avoid the seductive comfort of narrow-mindedness."

Uke steps in and grabs Tori's outer left arm sleeve (picture 1). Tori shifts back into right side forward Ichimonji no Kamae, striking Uke with an Ura Shuto to the right temple (picture 2). As Uke pulls Tori in, Tori steps online with Uke while wrapping his left arm around Uke's grabbing arm and sinks his knees to take Uke's balance (pictures 3-4). Tori stands up lifting Uke's arm up for shoulder lock (picture 5) and cross kicks Uke's right knee, taking him to the ground (picture 6).

Henka (Variation) #1 – Omote Oni Kudaki (Obvious Demon Crusher)

Uke grabs Tori's left lapel with his right hand (picture 1). Tori shifts back into right side forward Ichimonji no Kamae and applies an Ura Shuto to Uke's right Butsumetsu (picture 2). Tori shifts back into left side forward Ichimonji no Kamae as he applies Oni Kudaki lock. Be sure the hand near the wrist is palm up (pictures 3-6). Tori shifts back into right side forward Ichimonji no Kamae and lifts Uke's elbow, taking him to the ground (pictures 7-8).

合氣

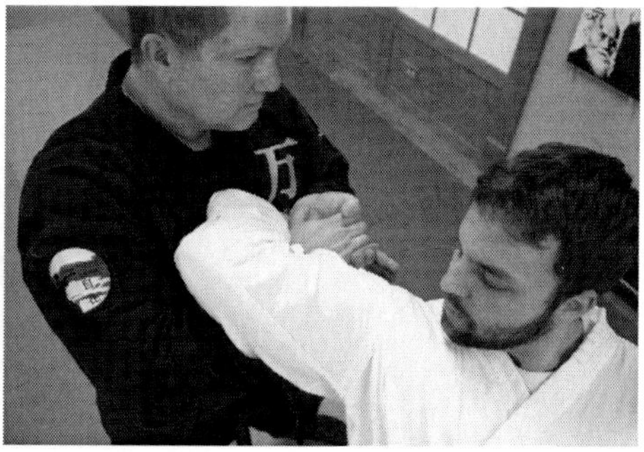

万全
合氣忍術

万全
合氣忍術

Henka #2 – Ura Oni Kudaki (Not-So-Obvious Demon Crusher)

Uke grabs Tori's left lapel with a right hand lunging grab (picture 1). Tori shifts into right side forward Ichimonji no Kamae while striking Uke with an Ura Shuto to his right temple (picture 2). Tori shifts back into left side forward Ichimonji no Kamae as he brings his forearm down in a rolling motion and rolls Uke's elbow up under Tori's chin for Oni Kudaki lock (pictures 3-4). Tori steps back into right side forward Ichimonji no Kamae, lifting his right elbow to take Uke to the ground (pictures 5-6).

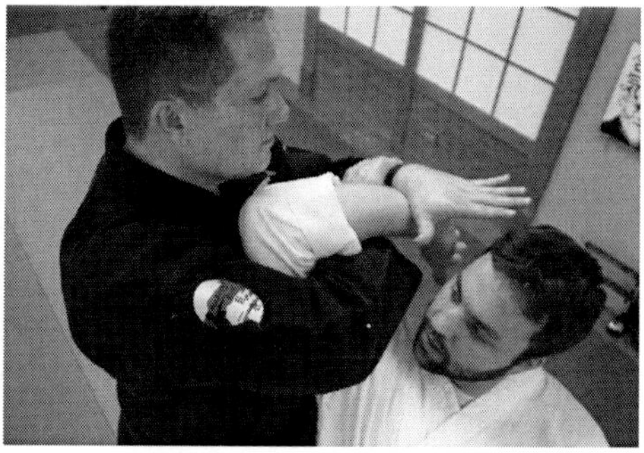

合氣忍術

合氣忍術

8. GANSEKI NAGE (Throwing a Big Rock)

Fit in – Variation: TE MAKURA (Hand Pillow)

In a physical encounter, the warrior must learn to not only enter and become skin tight but also fill up all available space. This will create Tsukuri, making it impossible for the attacker to continue his attack without unbalancing or injuring himself.

In life, the warrior must find ways to “fit in” to any situation. This is a way of not causing undue conflict or disrespect when he is in social or business situations. Learning to have no limitations is the goal of the warrior. He is able to adapt to whatever the situation demands. For example, the warrior is able to eat any food that is put before him, even if it is something that he would not order for himself. This lack of limitation keeps him from drawing unwanted attention and causing disrespect to other’s customs or preferences. The Banzenkan warrior has a history of being a ninja and must be able to “disappear” at will.

Uke comes in with a lunging right hand lapel grab. Tori steps back with the left foot and guides Uke’s arm in a clockwise motion grabbing the inside of Uke’s wrist, which is now outside (pictures 1-4). Tori steps in with his left foot and strikes Uke with a right-handed Ura Shuto to the right temple while placing Uke’s trapped wrist on the back of his neck (pictures 5-7). Tori hugs in Uke’s arm and pivots to the right, throwing Uke to the ground (pictures 8-10).

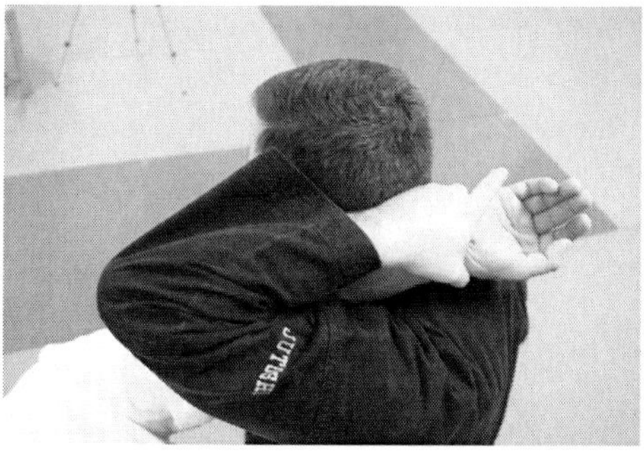

Henka – Te Makura (Hand Pillow)

Uke punches with a right-hand lunge punch and Tori steps inside of the punch, grabbing Uke's wrist on the inside (pictures 1-2). Tori then steps in with the right foot to place his instep against Uke's and his right arm under Uke's right arm, bringing Tori's right hand onto the back of his head (picture 3-4). Tori does a backward body drop while kicking upward with his right leg into a backward shoulder roll (pictures 5-7). Tori then applies an arm lock to pin Uke to the ground (picture 8).

The Banzenkan warrior student not only studies the principles from the Aiki Kihon Happo and Ninpo Kihon Happo, but he internalizes them so that he can use them in every technique he does. This takes years of practice. It is easy to understand the principles intellectually, but to ingrain them to the point where they can be used under stress, when the thinking brain cannot be accessed and the warrior is in survival brain mode, is the desired goal.

合氣忍術

合氣忍術

合氣忍術

合氣忍術

THE IMPORTANCE OF TRAINING SLOWLY

As a student begins to learn Aiki Ninjutsu in Skills & Drills class, he starts by breaking down the techniques into steps and moves very mechanically. This allows him to understand where to put his feet and how to move his hands. As he becomes more familiar with the technique, he begins to go a little faster and take away some of the "edges" that make the technique so mechanical.

As the student continues his training, he becomes more and more comfortable with the technique and begins to go faster and faster under varying levels of *Randori* or "free response." This begins to create a sense of confidence and belief that he can apply the technique in real life situations. The problem with this type of training is that the student starts to lose the correct mechanics needed to apply the technique on people other than a favorite training partner. The techniques begin to break down and the student continually adjusts by moving to another technique to finish off the attacker. This is an important skill to have, but not one that should be the default for a true warrior.

There are two types of masters in martial arts. One type is able to apply any technique to any attack that is given. This sounds easy but it VERY difficult. To be effective, the warrior must be able to set up the attacker, so that no matter what attack comes at them he falls into the technique that the warrior desires to apply. Masters never force their will or techniques onto an attacker, because they know that they cannot control anyone but themselves. If the attacker is larger and more aggressive, then it will be impossible for the warrior to move him to the space needed to apply the technique. To make it work, the warrior needs to set up the attacker by making him move into the space, so that the technique just fits in like a piece to a puzzle. This takes years of correct training. The training must consist of constant exploration, correction and refinement. This can only be done effectively at slow speeds. If the warrior only trains quickly, he will not learn to feel the subtle differences that are present and needed to control the situation.

The human brain learns by creating neural pathways. These create the ability to apply skills quickly and without "thought." This creates a habit or way of being. The secret to building these pathways is slow and concentrated corrective learning. When something breaks down in a technique or Randori, then the warrior must go back and fix it by doing the part over and over that failed. As the founder of Aiki Ninjutsu, Thomas Maienza said, "The technique never fails you, you fail the technique." By doing this concentrated learning, the warrior reinforces these neural pathways on that particular technique and this will allow the warrior to do the technique at a much faster speed with the proper mechanics. This requires consistent training, and the warrior is never done with going back and working on the basics, slowly and perfectly.

The other type of master is one who can adapt to any situation that comes without having a specific technique in mind. This is an even higher level of mastery and takes decades of failing and learning from those mistakes. This level is not accomplished by constantly "sparring" at high realistic speeds. It is internalized by learning how to recognize the failures and how to fix them so that techniques just happen in the midst of total chaos. Again, it is a long process of slowing things down and creating the neural pathways that make all techniques a way of the warrior's movement and not individualized techniques. This is when the warrior is able to get rid of the techniques that they have learned and just become the art itself.

FOUR STAGES OF A TECHNIQUE

Irimi

Irimi translates as "entering." In a technique, the warrior must enter and close the distance between himself and the attacker. This controlling of the space will create a situation where the assailant is not able to counter the warrior's technique. This is the first principle taught in Banzenkan Aiki Ninjutsu at the 9th Kyu or white belt level.

Tsukuri

Tsukuri is created when the warrior utilizes the irimi stage. The answer to the question, "How far do I enter?" is that the warrior must enter in until he is skin tight and fits into any available space. By doing this, the warrior will put the assailant in an off-balancing position so that he will fall or throw himself, if he attempts to counterattack. This is the first form of tsukuri.

The second form of tsukuri is understanding the mechanics of the lock or throw so that it is applied in a manner that will set the attacker up to injure himself, if he continues to attack. The idea is to apply the lock or throw at the correct angle for the future attack. If the assailant continues to attack, he will run into the technique, causing his own injury instead of the warrior's having to use force to apply the technique. This concept is internalized at the 3rd Kyu or red belt level of training.

Kuzushi

Kuzushi is the taking of balance. This can be done in three different ways; physical, mental and spiritual. Physical balance-taking is just like it sounds. The warrior moves his body in a way that takes their attacker's balance to a space of unbalance. If a person is fighting for balance he cannot effectively strike or throw with any power. The human mind will always adjust for balance first, making it virtually impossible for the attacker to finish his attack.

Mental balance taking is accomplished when the warrior does something to interrupt the attacker's plan. This can be done by moving at unexpected angles, changing up the timing in a technique or effective counterstrikes.

Spiritual balance taking occurs anytime the mind is deterred from its original mission. The best way to achieve this in a physical attack is by implementing Kosshi jutsu or pressure point attacks. These strikes or grabs send a "white-hot pain" through the assailant's body overriding his thought process and making him fear for his own safety. This overriding of the nervous system will make the assailant want to escape the incredible pain, taking away his will to continue the attack. This concept is internalized at the 2nd Dan or 2nd degree black belt level of training.

Kake

Kake is execution of the lock or throw. It is important that the warrior understand, that it may be impossible to apply a lock or throw to an attacker who is in balance and strong. To apply an effective technique, the warrior must utilize the first three steps before attempting to administer the desired defense. This will allow the warrior to be successful against much larger and stronger attackers, while not having to muscle the assailant and saving precious energy at the same time.

When the student is training and things seem to be falling apart, he should go back to these four stages and see if he is applying them correctly. By getting into the habit of fixing the technique through investigation and exploration, the warrior will internalize and eventually master the techniques to a point where they will require no thought, just "muscle memory."

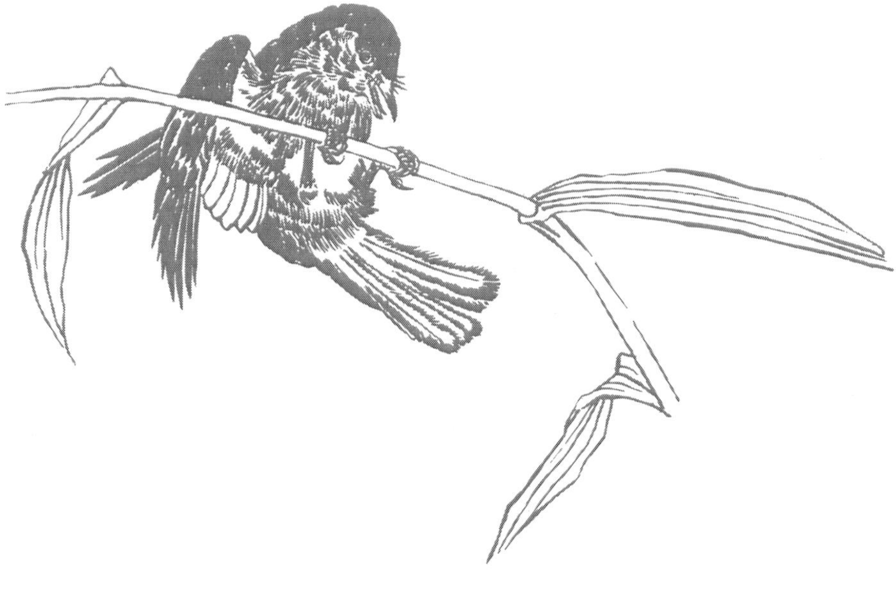

The arts that make up the curriculum of Banzenkan Aiki Ninjutsu all utilize sword work. For this reason, the warrior student begins his practice of the sword at white belt. The body movements required for proper sword cuts are the same movements that are used for the various strikes and throws that are found in the warrior's unarmed techniques. Learning to move the body as a whole unit, instead of just swinging the arms, is a key component to developing power.

KAMAE (Postures)

- *Daijodan no Kamae* ("Great Upper Posture")

- *Jodan no Kamae* ("Upper Posture")

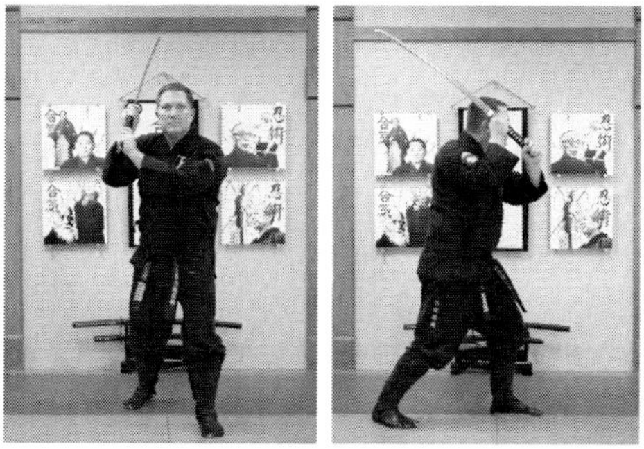

- *Hasso no Kamae* ("8 Aspects Posture")

- *Seigan no Kamae* (“Correct-Eye Posture”)

- *Gedan no Kamae* (“Lower Posture”)

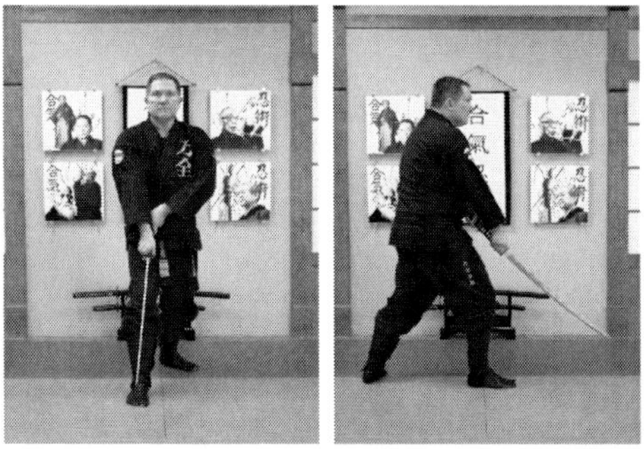

GIRI (Cuts)

- *Men Giri* (“Head Cut”; Vertical Cut)

• ***Kesa Giri*** ("Diagonal Cut")

• ***Do Giri*** ("Torso or Body Cut"; Horizontal cut)

Banzenkan students should practice all of the cuts from each kamae or posture.

WARM-UP DRILLS

- *Kiri Tsuke* ("Finishing Cut"; Cutting downward and sinking)

- *Ishi Wari* ("Stone Splitter Cut"; Rising and cutting downward)

GO GYO (FIVE FORMS)

As a white belt, the Aiki Ninjutsu student will study a set of five techniques called the ***Go Gyo*** or "Five Forms". These techniques are taught so that the student will begin to understand the basic defensive principles of Ninjutsu, which are to use: timing, angling, distancing and connection instead of force-on-force to defeat an opponent. Each of the Go Gyo represent one of the elements; Earth, Water, Fire, Wind and the Void. They all have a feeling of movement as well as a specific breathing pattern and Kiai or spirit yell that will help replicate the attitude associated with that particular technique.

These techniques should not be thought of as "self-defense" techniques but more as ***Tai Sabaki*** or body movement exercises. Once the techniques are learned and internalized, the student can use them as an efficient warm-up for further training.

- *Chi no Kata* (Earth Form)
  Breath = slow in / slow out – Kiai = vowel sound "Ah" or "Stop It!"

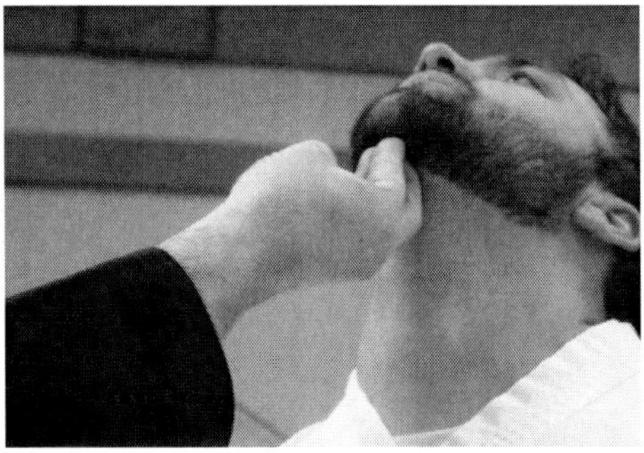

• *Sui no Kata* (Water Form)
Breath = slow in / fast out – Kiai = vowel sound "Oh" or "Whoa!"

- *Hi no Kata* (Fire Form)
  Breath = fast in / fast out – Kiai = vowel sound "Ā" or "Hey!"

- *Fu no Kata* (Wind Form)
  Breath = fast in / slow out – Kiai = vowel sound "Ē" or "Easy!"

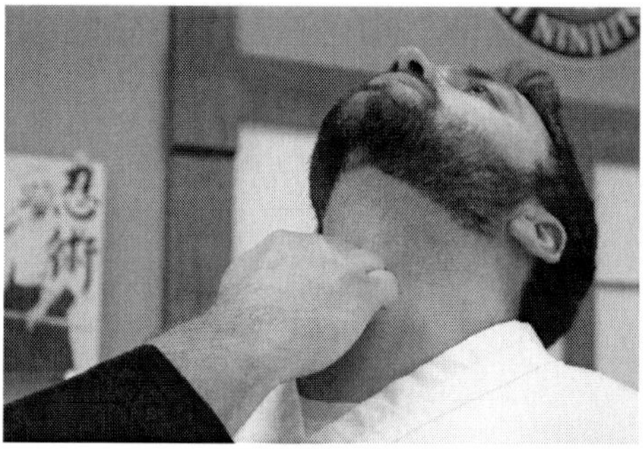

• *Ku no Kata* (Void Form)
There is no specific breath or vowel sound associated with this element

MUTO DORI SWORD DEFENSES

There are also three ***Muto Dori***, or unarmed against a sword, techniques that are taught at the white belt level. These also demonstrate the importance of correct angling, which effects the warrior's distance, timing and connection with the opponent. Again, these are not taught as self-defense techniques, but more as ***Tai Sabaki*** body movement exercises.

- ***Hira no Kata Muto Dori*** (Flat form unarmed against a sword)

• *Ichimonji no Kata Muto Dori* (Figure one form unarmed against a sword)

• *Jumonji no Kata Muto Dori* (Figure ten form unarmed against a sword)

KIME WAZA ROPPO

There are three sets of lock-ups that the Aiki Ninjutsu student internalizes. These are different ways to hold down an opponent once the warrior has taken him to the ground. Two of these sets come from the Ninjutsu side of our training. These are called ***Omote Gyaku Kime Waza Roppo*** and U***ra Gyaku Kime Waza Roppo***. The last set is taken from the Aiki systems that form the curriculum for Aiki Ninjutsu and is called the ***Aiki Kime Waza Roppo***.

The literal translation of ***Kime Waza Roppo*** is "six locking techniques." These three sets of locks will give the warrior eighteen different ways to effectively lock up an attacker to make sure he (the attacker) doesn't hurt himself or someone else. These locks are internalized and tested at the 7th Kyu orange belt level.

Omote Gyaku Kime Waza Roppo
(Six outer reversal locking techniques)

1

2

3

4

5

6

Ura Gyaku Kime Waza Roppo
(Six inner reversal locking techniques)

Aiki Kime Waza Roppo
(Six harmonious energy locking techniques)

1

2

3

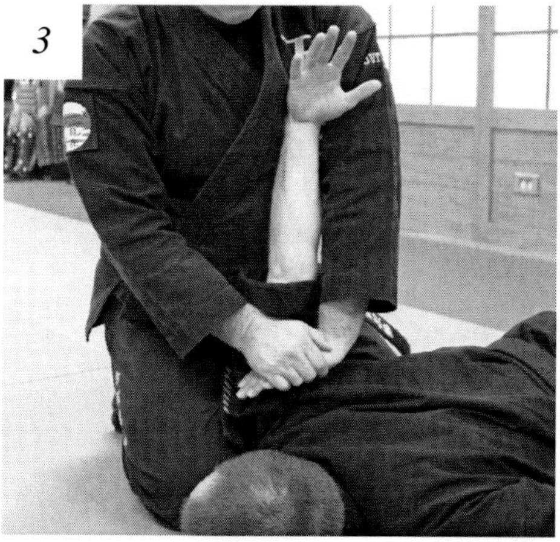

4

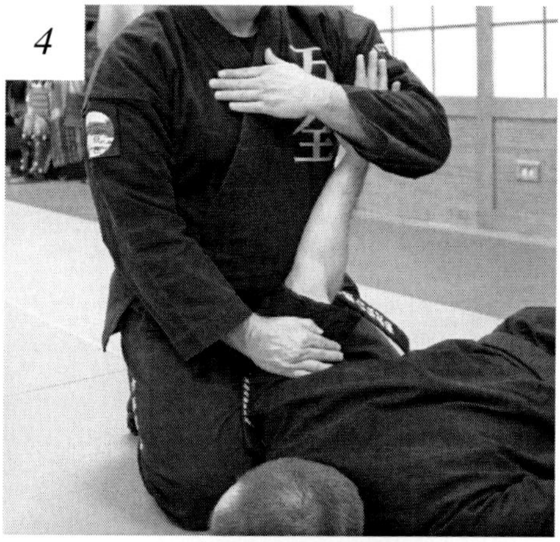

5

6

PRINCIPLES FOR DEALING WITH MULTIPLE ATTACKERS

In this section, we will look at the principles for dealing with more than one attacker, which teach that in a multiple attacker situation it is imperative that the warrior does not end up in the middle of the attack and that he must "Seek Shelter." These principles consist of 5 stages, "Slip, Stack, Rack, Slap and Wrap." Let us look at each step in more detail.

Slip

When the warrior finds himself in a situation where there is more than one attacker, he must be sure that he does not end up in the middle of the pack. It is almost impossible to fight three or more attackers at the same time when one is unarmed; add in knives or firearms and the situation can turn deadly in a heartbeat. For this reason, the warrior must first learn how to slip by the nearest attacker, "hiding" behind him, and using the attacker as a shield against the other assailants. Once behind the attacker, the warrior must take the attacker's balance so that he can be maneuvered in any direction needed. This can be done by grabbing the attacker at the elbow and neck and pushing his hips forward. This will give the warrior the control he needs to manipulate the "human shield." It is just as important to realize that there will come a time in the fight when the warrior will need to abandon the person he has control of and move to another "shield." In a multiple attacker situation, it is very important to keep moving and never stop. If the warrior does stop, he will be overwhelmed and end up fighting all of the attackers at once. This never ends well.

Stack

Once the warrior has taken a "shield", the next step is to stack the rest of the attackers. This can mean a couple of different things. First the warrior must line the attackers up so that they are in each other's way (as in the "Slip" example). This is called horizontal stacking. By employing this principle the warrior can help even the odds, giving him the opportunity to fight each attacker individually instead of all at once. On the street, attackers will not wait to attack individually, as in a Bruce Lee movie. It is more common for the warrior to end up fighting three or more assailants simultaneously. It is important when training that the student is put in real-life situations and not those found in movies, which were created to entertain an audience.

The second form of stacking is to apply a devastating technique to the "shield" putting him on the ground in front of the next attacker creating a barrier between the warrior and the others. When done correctly, the warrior can finish off the second attacker and stack him on top of the first downed attacker, creating a vertical stack.

Rack

Once the warrior has horizontally stacked the attackers, he can opt to rack them instead of stacking them. Racking is accomplished by using the body of the "shield" he is fighting as a weapon against the next attacker. This can be done by throwing him into their legs, thus injuring them and taking them out of the fight, so that the warrior can defend against another attacker or escape to safety.

Slap

While using an attacker as a shield the warrior must be alert to the location of all of the other assailants. As the warrior applies a devastating joint break or throw, he may have to strike incoming attackers to impede their process. This can be accomplished by using the warrior's limbs or by taking control of the "shield" and using the shield's hands, elbows and feet as weapons against their attacking buddies. This is much more difficult to accomplish under stress, and like all aspects of the secrets it must be practiced and internalized to be effective. Once it is mastered, though, it will give the warrior a great advantage when dealing with a deadly assault.

Wrap

The last step to these principles is probably the most difficult to learn. It involves taking control of the "shield" and tying up the next attacker's limbs with his. This will give the warrior the ability to break and incapacitate two or more attackers at once.

When dealing with multiple attackers, it is best to do quick and simple techniques that have been internalized. It is not the time for the flashiest techniques in a warrior's arsenal. Everything that is done should be geared to injuring the attacker immediately so that the warrior can escape. There is no place for ego or sportsmanship in a real life hostile encounter.

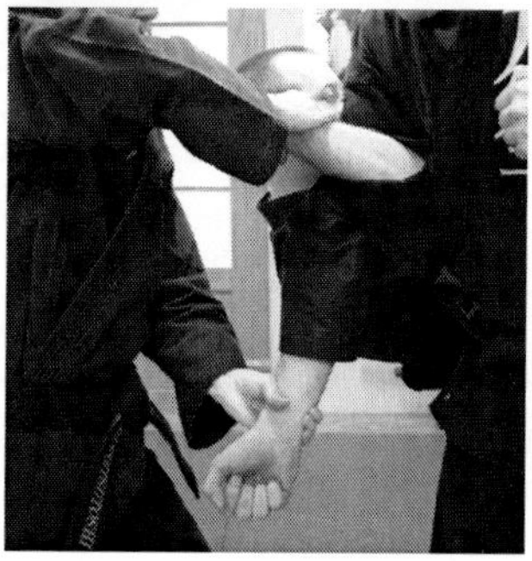

UNDERSTANDING THE ELEMENTS

One of the great martial art masters that inspired the art of Aiki Ninjutsu was Stephen K. Hayes. His contribution to the Ninjutsu martial arts helped make the art easier to understand for the Western mind. He made a correlation between Buddhist doctrine and martial technology, merging five elemental philosophies with the methods of self-protection. This system has been incorporated into his system of ***To-Shin Do*** as well as that of Soke Masaaki Hatsumi, ***Bujinkan Budo Taijutsu***.

There are five basic elements; Earth, Water, Fire, Wind and the Void. Everyone has a default elemental setting that dictates how he responds to situations, whether physical or mental. These default settings comprise what would be called someone's personality. It is important to understand that there is no element that is better than the others, and that all of the elements have a positive and negative side to them. By understanding how the elements relate to each other, the warrior is able to understand more fully why he reacts to the things around him the way he does. With this knowledge, the warrior can then understand why other people react to certain stimuli and make the decisions that they do. With lots of study, the warrior will be able to guide others so that they can achieve their goals or help the warrior achieve his without the person's knowing that he has been led in any way. This is the true art of the ninja, controlling the situation in a way that makes the other person feel that it was all his idea.

Chi – The Earth Element

The earth warrior is characterized by confidence, stability, dependability, and belief in self and ideals, standing strong in his convictions, like a mountain or a rooted tree. He tends to be concerned with the basic needs of life and is very security oriented, whether it is in his personal relationships, financial or family security. He tends to be a very tactile and hands-on person.

On the negative side, people who are primarily earthy can tend to be more closed minded, stubborn and less open to others' opinions. He can be more apt to remain in his daily routines and not seek change, even if it is for the better.

The element of earth is one of solid matter such as rocks, mountains, soil and trees. The earth characteristics of the human body are the bones and teeth. Warrior students train to use these tools in a defensive manner by utilizing punches, kicks, knee strikes, head butts, elbow strikes and biting.

In a self-defense situation, the warrior who is in the earth attitude will generate energy for striking or leverage, by using an up-and-down motion with the appropriate timing. This movement will create power allowing the warrior to hold his ground without having to rely on superior footwork. The warrior could find himself having to use an earth strategy even when he is not feeling like the biggest or strongest person in the altercation because the environment dictates that he do so. For example, if the warrior is up against a wall or car, in a narrow aisle such as in a plane or theater, or in a crowded space such as an elevator; the situation virtually demands an earth attitude. Another scenario might involve protecting someone else where the warrior has placed himself between that person and the threat and cannot move for fear of injury to the person they are trying to protect.

An example of how a warrior might defend himself using the earth energy principals can be seen in the following example. The warrior is at a restaurant with some friends when a man, who is stumbling drunk, begins to annoy them. The warrior tells him to go away, but instead the drunken man attacks. The warrior is not afraid because the man is too drunk to fight. At this level, the warrior would defend himself by using up-and-down motions with his body. He would not use back-peddling or attacking footwork, but simply stand his ground. The kamae used during this scenario would be a natural standing position. The warrior would not drop into a deep stance and try to intimidate the attacker. He would use basic strikes such as palm strikes, knees and elbows for his defense. The feeling of confidence comforts the warrior during this encounter. The energy is low.

In an argument, the warrior speaks from as deep a register as possible. He stands his ground simply using the facts to prove his point. Not getting emotional is the strength of the earth warrior.

In a relationship, trusting his partner is the warrior's strength. Feeling secure in the relationship and in his abilities satisfies his partner.

The earth level is truly basic, like dirt. With care, the warrior's earth energy can become like soil, ready to plant the seeds of living a fruitful life.

Sui – The Water Element

The water warrior exhibits curiosity, exploratory behavior and caution. The water warrior wants to understand the ins and outs of everything he does and about everyone he meets. He understands that making rash decisions can sometimes come with a heavy price.

On the negative side, the water person is one who may have a hard time making decisions. He tends to take too long to commit and may miss many great opportunities in life. The water warrior can also get in his own way by over-analyzing everything from a new martial arts technique to why his loved ones said what they did. Sometimes getting caught in one's own mind keeps the warrior from truly experiencing the world around them.

The water element should be thought of as waves on the ocean. The waves recede and then come back with more force. This motion of taking one's time and creating some space between himself and the problem allows him to come back with more effective and efficient solutions.

Fists associated with the water level are finger jabs and extended knuckle punches. These are used against muscles and nerves or pressure points, strategically causing "white hot" pain to the attacker, giving the warrior the time to apply a more devastating technique.

The water element in self-defense is best used when the warrior is feeling unsure or hesitant. In a real-life encounter, where serious injury or even death could be the result, it is not too hard to imagine the warrior's questioning his abilities or having reservations about having to seriously injure another human being. In this situation, the warrior would use 45° angling to stay safe while gathering information and opening up the attacker's targets for counterstrikes. Instead of using force, the warrior will take apart his opponent piece by piece until he is able to apply the final throw or lock up.

It is important that the warrior practice this attitude in the dojo by imagining he is terribly afraid of his training partner. This will give him a start point from which to work when he encounters it in real life. This is not an easy thing to replicate and it may take many sessions until the student is able to actually feel the fear and anxiety that he would feel on the street.

Here is a self-defense example. The warrior and a friend are standing in line at a grocery store, ready to make a purchase. A six foot six, three-hundred pound man behind them picks up a bottle and breaks it across the friend's face, then heads directly towards the warrior with a broken piece of glass in his hand. Because of the brutality and suddenness of the attack, the warrior is taken off guard and is still trying to figure out what is going on. He moves at 45° angles avoiding the attempted slashes and strikes pressure points on the attacker's arm, making him drop the weapon. He then uses angling to close the distance so he can apply a powerful takedown to subdue the much larger attacker.

It is important for the warrior to learn how to "fight smarter, not harder."

In an argument, the warrior thinks before responding, choosing his rebuttal carefully. Caution is his strength, seeking shelter and safety first.

In a relationship, he is very courteous, careful not to hurt any feelings, and sensitive. He wants to organize and set up dates and vacations, being sure to have all of the details figured out ahead of time with no surprises.

The water level is having fluid adaptability, in the warrior's techniques, in his personal life and in his heart.

Hi or Ka – The Fire Element

The fire warrior is generally extroverted, magnetic, passionate and charismatic. He is the one who stands out in a crowd, wanting to be the center of attention. He commands the room, doing his best to entertain everyone he meets. He tends to be goal-driven and have lots of self-discipline to turn those goals into reality.

The negative side of a fire person is that he may often be too quick to judgment and may make rash decisions without thinking through all of the things that might go wrong. This also applies to meeting people for the first time. He may tend to take people at face value only, and never get to know someone on a deeper level, preferring to talk about himself instead of learning about the other person. The fire warrior can become too obsessed with things like sports, hobbies, politics or religion, becoming die-hard "fans" of anything they find interesting.

The fire element in self-defense is being able to feel the urgency of a situation. Many martial art systems speak about trying to be mad or angry when they are in a fight. These systems rely on the adrenaline rush that is released when someone gets angry. Realistically, by the time someone gets angry and his adrenaline starts pumping, it is often too late. If it is a real confrontation, it's not going to last that long. Either the warrior will have been beaten or he will have been victorious, all in a matter of a few seconds.

Have you ever been in a car accident? How long after the accident did it take before your hands stopped shaking? Have you ever been in a heated argument? Did your hands shake? Has this happened every time you have been mad or in an argument? Sometimes our adrenaline kicks in right away and sometimes it takes a little while, sometimes not at all. The warrior cannot rely on this to give him the strength he needs to defeat the enemy.

Nobody should bank his family's safety on a theory. The warrior needs to train in consistencies. Without consistency in their training, the warrior will only have a false sense of safety.

For the Banzenkan student, the idea of fire should be viewed as having acute Isshin, initial connection, with the opponent. By becoming connected, the warrior will be able to sense the attacker's intention and move as the attacker "decides" to attack instead of waiting for the physical cues to start. This will give the warrior the ability to be physically slower than his opponent but fast enough to defeat a quicker opponent.

When referring to the fire urgency level, the warrior student must be sure not to confuse it with acting out of anger. A good example would be when the warrior realizes that a situation is escalating towards becoming a violent confrontation, and out of the corner of his eye, he sees several of the aggressor's friends getting out of a car. At this time, the warrior realizes that the opponent has been stalling. He can either react now or wait and deal with a half dozen opponents. The appropriate strategy would be to bring up the energy to the center of the warrior's chest, attack and escape.

When practicing martial art techniques, the warrior must also train on them from this urgent point of view. Instead of starting out standing in fighting stances facing each other, start out at opposite sides of the room. The training partners will walk towards each other, when in range Uke (opponent) will attack with a specific attack and then Tori (defender) will defend with the desired technique that has been assigned by the Sensei (teacher). This will feel very different. The student will more urgently feel the need to evade the strike.

Fists that would be used in this element are Shikan ken (extended knuckle fists), any poking type of fist, elbows and knees. Basically, the warrior will make the attacker run into bony parts of the body.

In an argument, the fire warrior will take a more powerful position, cutting the person off before he can express his side. The warrior sees the situation clearly and correctly telling the other person the way the situation is. The "my way or the highway" is the fire option.

In a relationship, the fire warrior takes an active part in planning events. He may even call his loved one and tell her what to wear and pick her up without telling her of his plans. The warrior is willing to do whatever it takes to make the relationship work.

Fu – The Wind Element

The wind warrior operates under compassion, harmony and love. These warriors live and dedicate their lives to helping others. He will often spend his extra time helping with charities that benefit the less fortunate, proper treatment of animals or protecting the environment. He tends to gravitate toward careers in medicine, teaching or humanitarian issues.

The negative side to the wind warrior is that he sometimes has a hard time standing up for himself as he does not want to cause waves or hurt anyone's feelings. He tends to bend to others wills instead of standing strong for his beliefs and desires. He is easily manipulated and sometimes tends to be naïve, as he wants to believe in the best of mankind.

The wind element in self-defense is characterized by circular movements and uses the "going around the problem" philosophy found in Sankyo, the third lesson. Other words that describe wind would be "Ju" (gentle or supple) and "Aiki" (harmonious energy).

The warrior student must learn to apply techniques gently and precisely to restrain the opponent. Take out all of the striking in practice, to focus on moving with, as opposed to moving against, the aggressor's force. Striking can and will interrupt the "flow" of the technique. This type of training will allow the warrior to use the minimum amount of force necessary to control the situation and stop the attacker from hurting himself or someone else.

Postures that apply to this element would be ones that do not appear threatening, to the aggressor or onlookers. The posture that the warrior takes will solicit an emotional response in the opponent. With this element, the warrior is careful to posture in a manner that shows vulnerability. This compassionate energy level is ideal for law enforcement.

In a relationship, someone operating from this level would take on some of his loved ones responsibilities, to make her day a little easier. Fulfilling his mate's needs and desires and making her happy is a high priority to the wind warrior.

In an argument, the modern wind warrior may decide to agree with the other side, just to avoid hurting feelings. The wind warrior listens to the other person's points very carefully, trying to understand.

Ku – The Void Element

This is the highest level of training. At this level, the warrior develops a "sixth sense" or intention sensing, being able to detect the intentions of an attacker before he moves physically. The warrior uses this ability in his physical protection methods as well as his personal life.

As a means of self-protection, a warrior who is fully actualized or awake will avoid danger and negativity through his actions. Psychically knowing danger is coming will give the warrior the ability to leave the restaurant before the gunman enters or deciding not to board the plane that will crash.

By using the correct words and carrying himself in the right manner, the warrior will not give an opponent an opportunity to attack. By not living in weakness, arguments don't happen and there is no conflict in his personal life. Meditation and communication with God or a higher self are done on a daily basis.

By understanding and training in all of the basic elements, the warrior will be able to use the appropriate element for the conflict and change as the situation dictates.

This moving from one element to the other creates the lack of an element, making it so the warrior is impossible to predict and impervious to the attacker's plans, giving him the skills to be invincible.

The warrior should practice every lock and throw found in the Aiki and Ninpo Kihon Happo from each of the elements. Understanding how the technique will change by how he is feeling will give him the experiences to internalize the techniques, so that the correct version will come out when he is put under stress. It is imperative that the warrior visualize and replicate the internal emotional connection to the element when practicing and not just think about being in a particular element. This is a skill that takes lots of practice. One way to do this is for the warrior to think back to a time where they felt the most confident (earth), intimidated or scared (water), angry or anxious (fire) and compassionate (wind). By using these historical reference points, the warrior will be able to feel the element inside of him, putting him completely in the attitude he is practicing.

The elements also teach the warrior how to relate to the other person he is encountering. If he is up against a larger, stronger physical opponent who is holding his ground, or trying to negotiate a deal with a close-minded or stubborn client, both earth element situations, the warrior should use a wind approach. Instead of standing in one place trying to stop the attacker's strikes and trading punches or continuously trying to push his point of view, he would go around the attacker's punches or arguments to find the source of the problem. In the physical encounter, the problem is the body, not the arms. By effecting the head and torso, he will end the onslaught of attacking limbs. In the negotiation, the warrior will go around the objections and look for the cause of the client's defensive attitude.

The opposite is also true. If the warrior finds himself dealing with an attacker who is bouncing and moving a lot, he should assume a strong kamae and become solid, striking strategically and powerfully as targets open up. His confidence in his techniques and skills will overcome the non-committed and erratic attacks of his opponent.

In a negotiation, it is important to know that when the warrior's facts are accurate and what is needed for the client, standing strong and being confident in his knowledge is the most professional thing he can do. Sometimes people, afraid of the unknown, will be elusive and will do their best to avoid a much-needed change.

So in review, earth can defeat wind just as wind can defeat earth, but trying to stand his ground and outlast a larger attacker or trying to evade an elusive attacker will not work in the warrior's favor no matter if it is a physical or mental battle.

For the warrior who comes up against a fiery and aggressive attacker committed to his destruction, the best response would be to use water angling to slow him down. By moving in an unpredictable manner while maintaining a safe distance, the warrior will be able to avoid the onslaught as well as open up the attacker's vulnerable targets. This strategy will allow the warrior to take the opponent apart piece by piece instead of trying to be faster and more aggressive than he is.

In negotiations, the warrior may find himself dealing with a person who is very passionate and committed to his beliefs, even though the facts do not support them. Instead of talking louder and trying to force his opinions down the client's throat, the warrior should instead take a water approach and listen to the opposing argument while changing the warrior's point of view to see openings that will allow him to approach the topic from a more advantageous position. By using phrases such as "I understand how you feel and I once felt that way too, but upon further investigation I found this might be an even better option" or "I can see why you would feel that way, but have you ever thought about this?", the warrior can get the client to start to see things from another point of view. When the warrior can get the client to feel like he came up with the solution on his own and it had nothing to do with the warrior than he has done an effective job.

The opposite is also true. When the warrior is dealing with an attacker who is not committed to the attack, the warrior should realize that something is not right and that danger is probably coming from another direction. If the person is between himself and the path to safety, the warrior needs to use a fiery hyper-connection (Isshin) and take the fight to the attacker. By using this connection, the warrior will be able to overpower the non-committed opponent and flee the situation.

In a negotiation, the warrior may find himself dealing with a person who is not committed to the process or outcome. The person is too obsessed with the minute details to see the bigger picture. If this happens, the warrior should use the fire strategy of beating down the client's objections with facts that support the warrior's position. By taking away the client's excuses the warrior can get him to commit to the agreement that is best.

In review, water can defeat fire just as fire can defeat water, but trying to overpower a much more aggressive attacker or continuously trying to be on the defense and never going on the offense will not work for the warrior. Assuming the appropriate element for the individual opponent is the key to being successful, whether on the battlefield or in the boardroom.

KYU RANK REQUIREMENTS

The following are the topics studied at each ***Kyu*** (color) belt level. These are to be internalized and understood to test for the next higher belt. The student is required to pass with an "A" grade. If his skill is not to that level, the instructor will inform him on exactly what he needs to improve on, so he can pass the next test.

9th Kyu (White Belt)

- Recite the Student Creed and first two sections of the Code of Mindful Action
- Ukemi (Rolls, Break-falls & Leaps)
- Name and show five of the Sixteen Treasure Fists
- Demonstrate a striking combination utilizing spinal twisting, bending of knees, Kiai and intention of hitting through the target
- Recite the names, translations, principles, technique names and translations for all of the Aiki Kihon Happo
- Demonstrate all of the Aiki Kihon Happo against a punching attack

8th Kyu (Yellow Belt)

- Recite the Student Creed and first three sections of the Code of Mindful Action
- Recite the names, translations and principles of all of the Ninpo Kihon Happo
- Demonstrate all of the Ninpo Kihon Happo on both sides
- Demonstrate a proficiency of keeping the back straight and knees bent (good balance) in basic Randori attacks

7th Kyu (Orange Belt)

- Recite the Student Creed and first four sections of the Code of Mindful Action
- Recite the names and translations of all three sets of Kime Waza Roppo
- Demonstrate all three sets of the Kime Waza Roppo
- Demonstrate a proficiency of being in the perfect position utilizing flow and supple power in basic Randori

6th Kyu (Purple Belt)

- Recite the Student Creed and first five sections of the Code of Mindful Action
- Explain verbally the Omote and Ura sides of Shomitsu and Sanmitsu

- Demonstrate a proficiency of connection and balance taking in basic Randori by utilizing Shomitsu and Sanmitsu
- Demonstrate a proficiency of disarming a knife attacker in basic Randori

5th Kyu (Blue Belt)

- Recite the Student Creed and first six sections of the Code of Mindful Action
- Explain verbally the Omote and Ura sides of Nimitsu and Yonmitsu
- Demonstrate a proficiency of controlling the distance in basic Randori by utilizing Nimitsu and Yonmitsu
- Demonstrate a proficiency of disarming a club attack in basic Randori

4th Kyu (Green Belt)

- Recite the Student Creed and first seven sections of the Code of Mindful Action
- Explain verbally the Omote and Ura sides of Gomitsu
- Explain the idea of "Ju"; gentle or supple movement
- Demonstrate a proficiency of supple movement and using the attacker's energy as well as attacking Uke's foundation in basic Randori when the attacker counters by utilizing Ju and Gomitsu
- Demonstrate a proficiency of disarming pistols and rifles from both front and back attacks

3rd Kyu (Red Belt)

- Recite the Student Creed and first ten sections of the Code of Mindful Action
- Explain verbally the idea of Tsukuri
- Demonstrate a proficiency in the 30 techniques of the ground flow drill
- Demonstrate a basic proficiency in Tsukuri in basic Randori
- Demonstrate the Kihon of the Hanbo to include basic Randori against unarmed attackers

2nd Kyu (Brown Belt)

- Recite the Student Creed and first twelve sections of the Code of Mindful Action
- Explain verbally the Omote and Ura sides of Rokumitsu
- Demonstrate proficiency of Rokumitsu in Randori

- Demonstrate proficiency of Randori under stress while wearing gear (helmet, chest protector and gloves)
- Demonstrate the Kihon of the Rokushakubo (six foot staff) to include basic Randori against sword attackers

1st Kyu (Brown with Black Stripe Belt)

- Recite the Student Creed and the entire Code of Mindful Action
- Explain verbally the Omote and Ura sides of Nanamitsu
- Demonstrate proficiency of Nanamitsu in Randori
- Explain the five principles of dealing with multiple attackers
- Demonstrate proficiency of dealing with up to three multiple attackers in Randori
- Demonstrate the Kihon of the Katana to include basic Randori against other sword attackers

SHODAN REQUIREMENTS

The following is the test for students taking their ***Shodan***, 1st degree black belt test, in the Banzenkan Aiki Ninjutsu system. All tests in the Banzenkan are 100% pass or fail tests designed to aid the student in mastery of the material at every level, which helps maintain integrity in the belt system.

Students must demonstrate verbal knowledge, including Japanese names, English translations and principles for each of the items listed below, as well as have competent physical skill in the following areas:

Aiki Kihon Happo

Ikkyo
Nikyo
Sankyo
Yonkyo
Gokyo
Rokkyo
Nanakyo
Hachikyo

Kime Waza Roppo

Omote Gyaku
Ura Gyaku
Aiki

Ninpo Kihon Happo

Ichimonji no Kata
Jumonji no Kata
Hicho no Kata
Omote Gyaku Dori
Omote Gyaku Tsuki
Ura Gyaku
Musha Dori
Ganseki Nage

Ninpo Kihon Variations

Hon Gyaku
Omote & Ura Oni Kudaki
Te Makura

16 Treasure Fists

Kikaku-ken
Shuki-ken
Fudo-ken (Kongo-ken)
Kiten-ken (Shuto-ken)
Shishin-Ken
Shito-Ken (Boshi Ken)
Koppo-Ken
Ryu-Ken
Shako-Ken
Goshi-Ken
Shikan-Ken
Happa-Ken
Sokki-Ken
Sokuyaku
Sokugyaku
Tai-ken

7 Warrior Secrets

Shomitsu
Nimitsu
Sanmitsu
Yonmitsu
Gomitsu
Rokumitsu
Nanamitsu

Go Gyo

Chi no Kata
Sui no Kata
Hi no Kata
Fu no Kata
Ku no Kata

Ukemi

Rolling
Break Falls
Leaps

Unarmed Kamae

Seiza
Fudoza
Shizen no Kamae
Bobi no Kamae
Hicho no Kamae
Ichimonji no Kamae
Doko no Kamae
Seigan no Kamae
Jumonji no Kamae
Kosei no Kamae
Hira no Kamae
Hoko no Kamae

Hanbo (half-staff) Kihon

Ritsu Rei
Za Rei
Shizen no Kamae
Hira Ichimonji no Kamae
Yoko Hira Ichimonji no Kamae
Issen no Kamae
Musha Dori
Ganseki Nage
Muso Dori
Hon Gyaku
Kick Defenses
Ken Uchi
2-Handed Sliding Uchi
1-Handed Uchi
Tension Uchi

Ken (sword) Kihon

Ritsu Rci
Za Rei #1
Za Rei #2
Dai Jodan no Kamae
Jodan no Kamae
Hasso no Kamae
Seigan no Kamae
Ichi no Kamae
Kasumi no Kamae
Chudan no Kamae
Gedan no Kamae
To Sui no Kamae
Jiziri Gedan no Kamae
Ryu Sui no Kamae
Hasso Uchi
Niji Uchi
Ashi Uchi
Sho Men Giri
Kesa Giri
Gyaku Kesa Giri
Do Giri
Ashi Giri
Tsuki
Sho Men Giri Batto Noto
Do Giri Batto Noto
Kihon Sword Flow Drill

Bo (staff) Kihon

Ritsu Rei
Za Rei
Hira Ichimonji no Kamae
Yoko Hira Ichimonji no Kamae
Ten Chi Jin no Kamae
Gyaku Ten Chi Jin no Kamae
Ten Chi no Kamae
Seigan no Kamae
Chudan no Kamae
Gedan no Kamae
Ukemi
Men Uchi
Tento Men Uchi
Yoko Men Uchi (3 styles)
Do Uchi
Kote Uchi
Ashi Barai / Sune Uchi
Suso Haneage
Tsuki
Tachi / Yoko Furi
Go Ho Kata
Ura Go Ho Kata

Jutaijutsu

30 Technique Ground Flow Drill

Randori "Free Response"

Students will perform 10 minutes of Randori against unarmed attackers, multiple attackers and knife attacks. During this portion, students will have to show the "Secrets" under free response circumstances. Students must also have attended at least one Shugyo, austere training, weekend, as well as 6 seminars to qualify for their Shodan test.

GLOSSARY OF DOJO TERMS

吾勝 *Agatsu*: "Self-victory"

合気 *Aiki*: "Harmonious energy or interaction"

合気道 *Aikido*: "The way of harmony with universal energy"

足 裁き *Ashi Sabaki*: "Footwork"

当身 *Atemi*: "Striking the body"

万全 *Banzen*: "Perfection or flawlessness"

万全館 *Banzenkan*: "Hall of perfection or flawlessness"

木剣 *Bokken*: "Wooden sword"

武道 *Budo*: "Martial way"

仏滅 *Butsumetsu*: "Buddha is destroyed." The nerve running along the third rib on the sides and around the front of the body

地 *Chi*: "Earth"

中段 *Chudan*: "Middle position"

段 *Dan*: "Black belt rank"

道 *Do*: "Way/path"

道場 *Dojo*: "Place of the way"; school

道場 長 *Dojo Cho*: "The head of the dojo"

どうも 有難う 御座いました *Domo Arigato Gozaimashita*: "Thank you very much"

道主 *Doshu*: "Hereditary head"

風 *Fu*: "Wind"

不動心 *Fudo Shin*: "Immovable mind"

下段 *Gedan*: "Lower position"

五蜜 *Gomitsu*: "Fifth secret"; secret of attacking the foundation

袴 *Hakama*: "Divided skirt like pant"

八方 *Happo*: "Eight directions / infinite"

八双の構え *Hasso No Kamae*: "Eight aspects posture"

変化技 *Henka Waza*: "Variation of technique"

本部道場 *Hombu Dojo*: "Head, lead or central dojo of an organization"

左 *Hidari*: "Left"

入身 *Irimi*: "Entering"

一心 *Isshin*: "One mind"; initial connection

上段 *Jodan*: "Upper position"

火 *Ka* or *Hi*: "Fire"

構え *Kamae*: "Posture or stance"

神座 *Kamiza*: "A small shrine located the front of the dojo"

館長 *Kan-cho*: "Head of the organization"

型 *Kata*: "Pattern of movement"

固め技 *Katame Waza*: "Hold downs or pinning techniques"

刀 *Katana/To*: "Samurai sword / blade"

剣 *Ken*: "Sword or blade"

氣 *Ki*: "Spirit, energy or intention"

気合 *Kiai*: "Spirit or energy yell"

基本 *Kihon*: "Fundamental"

後輩 *Kohai*: "A junior student"

心 *Kokoro/Shin*: "Heart or mind"

呼吸 *Kokyu*: "Breath"

骨指術 *Kosshi Jutsu*: "Attacking with fingers/knuckles; pressure point attacks"

空 *Ku*: "Emptiness or void"

崩し *Kuzushi*: "Destroying the opponent's balance, mentally, physically and spiritually"

級 *Kyu*: "Color belt levels of belt rank"

間合い *Ma ai*: "An interval, meaning distance relative to time"

前 *Mae*: "Front or forward"

正勝 *Masakatsu*: "True victory."

右 *Migi*: "Right"

無心 *Mushin*: "No mind"

結び *Musubi*: "Harmonious interaction"

流れ *Nagare*: "Flowing"

投げ *Nage*: "A person executing the throwing technique"

七蜜 *Nanamitsu*: "Seventh secret"; controlling the space (Kukan)

二蜜 *Nimitsu*: "Second secret"; secret of using the natural tendency of the human eyes to track

忍 *Nin*: "Perseverance"

忍者 *Ninja*: "Person who perseveres"

忍術 *Ninjutsu*: "Art of perseverance"

帯 *Obi*: "Belt"

表 *Omote*: "Outer or obvious"

お願いします *Onegaishimasu*: "Please assist me", this is said by and to the instructor when opening class and to the student's training partner before a technique is practiced

乱取り *Randori*: "Free-response training"

礼儀 *Reigi*: "Observance of proper etiquette"

六蜜 *Rokumitsu*: "Sixth secret"; secret of creating a dramatic pause

三蜜 *Sanmitsu*: "Third secret"; secret of connection

先生 *Sensei*: "Teacher"

先輩 *Sempai*: "Senior student"

師範 *Shihan*: "Master instructor"

死角 *Shikaku*: "Dead space or angle"

膝行 *Shikko*: "Knee walking"

初段 *Shodan*: "Initial level", used to denote first degree black belt

正面 *Shomen*: "Front or top of head"

初蜜 *Shomitsu*: "Initial Secret"; secret of direction of balance

修行 *Shugyo*: "Austere training"

外 *Soto*: "Outside."

水 *Sui*: "Water"

捨て身 *Sutemi*: "To throw-away the body or to sacrifice"

座り技 *Suwari Waza*: "Performing a technique from a seated position"

太刀 *Tachi*: "Long curved Japanese sword usually used from horseback"

立ち技 *Tachi Waza*: "Standing techniques"

体術 *Taijutsu*: "Art of using the body"

体裁き *Tai Sabaki*: "Body movement"

短刀 *Tanto*: "Knife"

転換 *Tenkan*: "Turning the body 180 degrees"

転身 *Tenshin*: "Uke retreats 45 degrees away from the attack (water footwork)"

取り *Tori*: "Taking", the person doing the technique

突き *Tsuki*: "Thrust"

作り *Tsukuri*: "Lock up", getting a person locked up so that they cannot continue to attack

内 *Uchi*: "Inside."

内弟子 *Uchi Deshi*: "A live-in student"

受け *Uke*: "One who receives the technique"

受身 *Ukemi*: "Receiving with the body"

裏 *Ura*: "Inner or less than obvious"

後ろ *Ushiro*: "Backwards or behind"

技 *Waza*: "Technique"

四蜜 *Yonmitsu*: "Fourth secret"; secret of spinal alignment

横 *Yoko*: "Side or sideways"

横面 *Yokomen*: "Side of the head"

残心 *Zanshin*: "Remaining mind"

ABOUT THE AUTHOR

Michael Jutoshi Eichenberg

Mr. Eichenberg has dedicated his life to the study of self-protection. He currently holds a 3rd degree black belt in To-Shin Do and a 7th degree black belt in Aiki Ninjutsu. He is the Founder of Banzenkan Aiki Ninjutsu and the Co-founder of PAPA (Pilipinas Aikido Propagation Association) Aikido USA. He began his training in Ninjutsu with Stephen K. Hayes and Jack Hoban. He is currently the student of Aikido Master, Sensei Johnny Tenegra.

He has also served as USMC Security Forces and as a member of an executive protection team. He is currently the owner of Warrior's Edge Martial Arts in Naperville, Illinois.

Thanks to everyone who selflessly gave their time to help create this book.

Special thanks to Kent TeVault for editing the text and teaching me proper grammar that will help me finish the next book much quicker. Thanks to Len Deptula for taking the pictures to help me get my point across even better and to Karri Rahkonen for putting the book together in a format that makes it easy for the student to follow and also for the great cover art work.